OZZY @75

Daniel Bukszpan

INTRODUCTION

In 2005, *Esquire* ran a feature called "What I've Learned," in which Ozzy Osbourne, then fifty-six, talked about some of the epiphanies he's had in his life. In addition to "I can't do anything in moderation" and "You don't accidentally become an asshole," he made another statement that no one can argue with.

"Nobody else in the world fucking sounds like me."

This is accurate. Deep Purple's Glenn Hughes, a world-class singer who briefly fronted Black Sabbath in 1986, said as much in a 1995 interview with journalist Steve Rosen. Hughes said that even though that job included singing songs originally sung by the much more technically adept Ronnie James Dio, the Ozzy stuff gave him the most problems.

"It wasn't so hard singing the Dio stuff," he said. "It was fucking really, really hard singing Ozzy Osbourne songs because nobody sounds like Ozzy . . . Ozzy Osbourne is Ozzy Osbourne and it works for him."

Hughes was right then, and he's right now. Ozzy Osbourne has one of the most distinctive, immediately recognizable voices in rock music. He's always sounded like Ozzy, no matter which musicians or producers he was working with. And whether he's singing a piano ballad or being backed up by the loudest musicians in heavy metal, Ozzy always sounds like Ozzy, and it always works.

Everyone already knows the broad strokes of his life. Born into poverty, he escaped his circumstances by becoming the lead singer for Black Sabbath. He became even more popular as a solo act, something not always guaranteed when a band member steps out on their own. That alone would be remarkable, but he expanded his celebrity status by appearing on MTV's *The Osbournes*, which made him the most unlikely of TV dads.

His career trajectory has been like no other that I've ever witnessed. As a member of Generation X, I was too young for Black Sabbath when he was the singer. When the 1973 classic *Sabbath Bloody Sabbath* was released, the only record I owned was a 45-rpm single sung by *Sesame Street*'s Cookie Monster. Ozzy got on my radar as a solo artist instead when other kids in my high school would speak in fearful, hushed tones about this man who bit the head off a bat.

To thirteen-year-old me, Ozzy Osbourne was a demonically possessed lunatic first and foremost, and the fact that he was also a musician was almost a side issue. But once I heard *We Sold Our Soul for Rock 'n' Roll*, I was hooked. Ozzy Osbourne has never left high rotation for me, and barring some extensive brain injury, I don't see it ever happening.

This book comes just after a February 1, 2023 announcement on his official Instagram account saying that due to a 2019 accident that damaged his spine, he is no longer be able to tour. For a lot of artists, that would be the end of the story, but less than a week later, he won two Grammy awards—best rock album for *Patient Number 9* and best metal performance for the song "Degradation Rules." So yet again, in typical Ozzy fashion, an event that should have ended his career was instead followed by a huge triumph.

Considering all of the potentially fatal things he's done in his life, it's not hyperbole to say it's a miracle that he's now seventy-five years old. However, despite his advancing age, no one should write him off. Few musicians have been written off as many times as Ozzy Osbourne, and the people who did it were wrong every time. So until his death is confirmed by the Associated Press, medical authorities, his family, or all of the above, don't bet against him. He's not going anywhere.

Ozzy channels Jim "Dandy" Mangrum's wardrobe during the *Diary of a Madman* album cover shoot.

PART 1

OZZY ZIG SEEKS GIG, 1948—1969

Ozzy at Germany's Star Club in 1969, when Black Sabbath was still known as Earth.

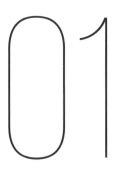

01

"I WAS THE CRAZY GUY"

A HOUSEHOLD NAME IS BORN

DECEMBER 3, 1948

Hell (pictured), also known as 14 Lodge Road in Aston, Birmingham, where Ozzy was raised.

The Birmingham tram in 1956 may not have seemed that spectacular to an eight-year-old Ozzy, but one day, one of them would be named after him.

Ozzy Osbourne was born John Michael Osbourne on December 3, 1948, to John and Lilian Osbourne. Although he would become one of Birmingham's favorite sons by growing up in the Aston area, his birth certificate says that his family resided in Kingstanding when he was born.

Aston was a working-class suburb, and everyone in Osbourne's life worked blue-collar jobs, including his future Black Sabbath bandmates. He grew up poor in a family of eight and remembered his parents constantly fighting about money. It was a harsh environment to grow up in, and the future singer had his share of tribulations to deal with.

"I'm extremely dyslexic, but they didn't understand then what dyslexia was," he told The Big Issue in 2014. "I went to school, a secondary modern in Birmingham, where there were 49 kids in a class, all boys. The kids used to mess around, smoking behind the toilets."

School wasn't the only place where a young John Michael Osbourne faced challenging situations. In 2003, he told Entertainment Weekly that when he was eleven years old, he was repeatedly sexually assaulted by bullies.

"Two boys used to wait for me to come home after school," he said. "It became a regular thing on the way home from school. It seemed to go on forever."

Osbourne said that he never told his family about what happened. In 1959, he said, it just wasn't discussed.

"When I was a kid, people did not talk about these things like they do now," he said. "You didn't have chat shows talking about child molestation."

While Osbourne's childhood was traumatic, he emerged from primary school with one thing that would serve him well for the rest of his life. In his 2010 memoir, I Am Ozzy, the singer said that he had picked up the nickname "Ozzy" during childhood, and it stuck.

It may have only been intended as a way of differentiating him from all the other "Johns" that he likely went to school with, but it went on to become a household name, one that didn't necessarily need a surname after it. Just like with Cher and Madonna, you can refer to him just as "Ozzy," and everyone knows who you're talking about.

However, before becoming a household name, he would first have to survive school. He told The Big Issue that he used humor to smooth over his rough social interactions. Being a bit of a class clown type gave him a way of coping.

"I was the crazy guy," he explained. "I made the big tough guys like me by making them laugh."

His sense of humor and natural showmanship helped him get through the school day, but there was still the matter of what he would do once he graduated. There were very few options for people living in Birmingham, and he wasn't interested in pursuing any of them.

"Birmingham wasn't and isn't a very rich area," he told NY Rock in 2002. "It was rather dreadful, and everybody in my family worked in factories, really mindless jobs that were physically exhausting. My father, my mother, my sisters, they all worked in factories in Birmingham."

Osbourne knew that he didn't want to follow this path, but he was initially resigned to it and would make a few attempts at doing blue-collar work in adulthood. Before then, though, something else would happen that showed him there might be a better way . . .

02

THE LONG AND WINDING ROAD

OZZY HEARS HIS FUTURE ON THE RADIO

AUGUST 23, 1963

When Ozzy Osbourne was a teenager, a seismic event took place that permanently altered the trajectory of his life. He heard a group called the Beatles singing "She Loves You" on his transistor radio, and he told *Esquire* that was the moment when everything changed for him. He didn't decide to become a musician at that precise second, but he never looked at things the same way again.

"When I heard 'She Loves You,' my world went up like a shooting star," he said. "It was a divine experience. The planets changed. I used to fantasize that Paul McCartney would marry my sister."

While his sister failed to marry any member of the Beatles, there was still no un-hearing the music for him and no way to put his desire to become a musician back in the bottle. In 2019, he told *Blabbermouth* that his son Jack had asked him why he had gone so bonkers for them.

"The only way I can describe it is like this," he said. "'Imagine you go to bed today, and the world is black and white, and

then you wake up, and everything's in color. That's what it was like!'"

Today, it may be hard to fathom how one chirpy pop group could have such a significant effect on vast swaths of people, but that's precisely how it was. Osbourne told *NY Rock* in 2002 that everything your parents hated about the Beatles was what had made him love them.

"They were my first addiction," he said. "I could switch off, forget my surroundings and dive into the music. It was something magical, almost a spiritual experience for me. Of course, my dad hated it. Way back then, the Beatles were revolutionaries, and their music was revolutionary music. You know, they were considered to be a bad influence because they gave the kids ideas, the ideas to do something else with their lives than waste it in factories or become plumbers. For adults, it was a dangerous thing. But for us, they were heroes."

Many musicians of Osbourne's vintage have said the same thing about the Fab Four, and many of those who were inspired to pick up a guitar because of "She Loves You" would venture into similarly poppy territory. Unfortunately for Osbourne, the Summer of Love never made it to the economically depressed, industrial part of England that he called home. As the concise two-minute pop of the Beatles' early catalog gave way to music more in tune with the hippie ethos, he found he just couldn't relate.

"Back in the day, it was, 'If you're going to San Francisco, be sure to wear some flowers in your hair,'" he told *Esquire*. "Where in the fuck was San Francisco?

And the only flowers we ever saw in Aston were on a coffin going to a cemetery."

As the 1960s waned, a new crop of musicians appeared who had one foot in flower power and the other in a primitive sludge that would one day be known as heavy metal. Bands like Iron Butterfly, Vanilla Fudge, and Deep Purple were technically psychedelic groups when they emerged in the 1960s, but they all incorporated guitar distortion and pounding drums in ways that pointed the way to something darker. Even the Beatles themselves had recorded "Helter

Skelter" and "I Want You (She's So Heavy)," songs that seemed to suggest that they too were sick of all the hippie shit.

A couple of years later, Ozzy Osbourne and three of his fellow Brummies would unite to create a darker, heavier, and more antisocial sound than anything that had come before. But without that fateful moment of hearing "She Loves You" for the first time, none of it would have happened.

Beatlemania shrieks and faints its way into Birmingham in 1963. Ozzy soon came down with a case of it himself, making him permanently unfit for some desk job.

03

"A BIT OF BURGLARY"

OZZY VS. GAINFUL EMPLOYMENT

WINTER 1966

Could this be some of Ozzy's handiwork from when he was employed at a slaughterhouse?

After leaving school, Osbourne resigned himself to securing the sort of employment he believed he was condemned to. He embarked on a series of blue-collar jobs in an attempt to conform to what was expected of him, but it never worked out. He may have wanted to fit in, but his employers had other plans.

"My dad thought I should become a tradesman, to get a chance and better myself, get away from the factories, you know," he told *NY Rock* in 2002. "So when I finished school, I tried to become a plumber. It didn't work out; it wasn't for me. Then I tried to become a bricklayer. It didn't work out. Then I tried to be a construction worker—same story. Everything I tried seemed to be doomed. I hated it, got sick of it really quick."

He did hold one job that he claimed to enjoy—working at a slaughterhouse. In 2016, he told *Metal Hammer* that he didn't

necessarily enjoy it because he got to kill animals, although that theory would tie in nicely with the traumas he would visit upon innocent doves in later decades. Rather, he liked it because of the flexible hours and competitive salary.

"When you'd finished the kill, you could go home," he said. "You'd get there at six in the morning and, depending on how many cattle you had to kill, sometimes you'd be back home three or four hours later. So you had the rest of the day off. That was better than working nine to five in an office. When you finished the kill, you could go home, and that's what I liked about it. The money was good as well."

The abattoir job aside, Ozzy Osbourne and the workplace generally did not play well with each other. He said that, in general, he had a hard time staying employed, and it caused him plenty of stress at home.

"I couldn't hold a job down," he told *The Big Issue*. "I was always being yelled at by my mother for not bringing any money into the house."

He would eventually leave home, but by his own admission, he didn't really have anywhere in mind to go. He would soon find himself committing petty crimes, but thankfully, he had a very brief career in that field because he was as good a thief as he was a plumber, a bricklayer, or a construction worker.

"I tried a bit of burglary, but I was no good at that," he said. "Fucking useless. I didn't do any major burglary jobs. It was less than three weeks before I got caught. My dad said to me, that was very stupid. And I did feel very stupid."

The lesson could have ended there if Osbourne had just paid his fine, but for whatever reason, he didn't, and he ended up getting thrown in jail. Furthermore, his father wouldn't pay the fine to get him out because he had wanted to teach his wayward son a lesson. It must have worked because Osbourne was never again a guest of the British penal system. Not for stealing, anyway.

"That was a short, sharp lesson," he said. "It certainly curbed my career in burglary."

Stock photo of Winson Green Prison in Birmingham in 1958. Less than a decade later, Ozzy would do a six-week stint for his youthful indiscretions.

WELCOME TO THE POLKA TULK BLUES BAND

JOHN MICHAEL OSBOURNE JOINS THE MUSIC BUSINESS

DECEMBER 11, 1968

It has been said by a great many that the way to get to Carnegie Hall is to "practice, practice, practice." It has also been said that to run a successful retail establishment, you need three things— "location, location, location." But if you're Ozzy Osbourne and you want to become a full-time musician, all you need is a microphone and a PA.

"If my father hadn't bought me a microphone when I was 18, I definitely wouldn't be here now," he told *The Big Issue.* "He bought me a microphone, and it was shortly after that I met the guys who would become Sabbath. It was the fact that I had my own microphone and PA system that got me in the band. If I hadn't had them, I would never have got the gig."

Ozzy's father buying him a microphone and PA system was a gesture that amounted to a lot more than just a father helping out his kid. That equipment was not cheap, certainly not by the standards of a Birmingham factory worker. Still, he understood his son's passion for music and desire to break into it. He bit the bullet and made the sacrifice, as Osbourne told *Blabbermouth* in 2019, and the singer understood what a big one it had been for his dad.

"My father was a factory worker who wouldn't miss a day's work if his life depended on it," Osbourne said. "He worked the night shift. He knew the passion I had for the music . . . and he went into debt for me. It was $500 or something like that. We couldn't afford it, but he bought me a PA system and a microphone."

With his microphone and PA in hand, Osbourne joined forces with bassist Terrence "Geezer" Butler in the band Rare Breed, but it was not to be, mainly because Osbourne was "really annoyed" by the guitar player, as he told *NY Rock* in 2002. This prompted the singer to post a sign in a local record store proclaiming, "Ozzy Zig Seeks Gig." But who is this "Ozzy Zig" anyway?

"I used to call myself Ozzy Zig because I thought it sounded cool, and I thought everybody would start asking who Ozzy Zig was," Osbourne said.

Guitarist Tony Iommi and drummer Bill Ward, formerly of the blues band Mythology, responded to the ad. Iommi remembered Osbourne from their school days, and his memory of the singer was not necessarily 100 percent

favorable. Still, the foursome ended up joining forces under the name the Polka Tulk Blues Band. That name sucked, so they changed it to Earth, but there was already another band called Earth performing gigs elsewhere in England.

This situation called for a new name for the band, one that would be iconic, memorable, and most importantly, not in use by someone else. However, it almost went down the toilet when guitarist Iommi announced that he was leaving the band to join Jethro Tull.

It didn't last. In fact, it lasted less than a month. Jethro Tull was successful but Iommi came running back to the band, even though staying with them might have been the safer bet. Regardless, he returned to the band, and the foursome set about trying to figure out their new name.

Ozzy Osbourne and Tony Iommi summon Pazuzu in Germany during one of their last performances as Earth.

===⬡===⬡===⬡===⬡===⬡===⬡===

WHAT IS THIS THAT STANDS BEFORE ME?

The poster for the 1963 Mario Bava horror movie *Black Sabbath*, which four miscreants from Birmingham took as their band name. It certainly rolls off the tongue better than the original title, *I Tre Volti Della Paura*.

===⬡===⬡===⬡===⬡===⬡===⬡===

OZZY AND HIS BAND SCARE OFF THE HIPPIES

===⬡===⬡===⬡===⬡===⬡===⬡===

AUGUST 9, 1969

In 1969, the band formerly called Earth that had formerly been called the Polka Tulk Blues Band found themselves at a crossroads. They needed to pick a new name, and while they were at it, they thought their musical style could use a shake-up too.

Osbourne said that the band took inspiration for their new name from the marquee over the movie theater across the street from their rehearsal space. He said that most of the time, the theater played horror movies, and while some might think that genre might scare people away, it had the opposite effect. People liked to be scared and would wait in an orderly line to pay for the privilege.

The band wondered if the same principle might apply to music. Maybe people would want to hear a band whose music was the sonic equivalent of a horror movie? They certainly had nothing to lose by trying, and it wasn't exactly a popular style with lots of competition. If anything, they could corner the market.

Bassist Geezer Butler was a fan of author Dennis Wheatley, whose books, such as 1934's *The Devil Rides Out*, often focused on black magic and the occult. The bassist took inspiration from the books and from a vision of a ghostly entity that he had one night as he lay in bed. Those elements inspired him to collaborate with Osbourne on a new, sinister piece of music that represented a permanent break from the Polka Tulk years.

The song was named after the 1963 Mario Bava horror movie *Black Sabbath*. It sounded like nothing that had ever come before it. Played at a painfully slow tempo and using the unusual musical interval known as the "tritone," the music perfectly fits the lyrics. The lyrics are among the few that Osbourne helped write with Butler, otherwise the band's full-time lyricist. The words made reference to Butler's supernatural visitor.

WHAT IS THIS THAT STANDS BEFORE ME? FIGURE IN BLACK WHICH POINTS AT ME TURN 'ROUND QUICK AND START TO RUN FIND OUT I'M THE CHOSEN ONE

Those lyrics plus that music equaled the clearest evidence yet that the hippie revolution was over, and the hippies had lost. In fact, no less an authority than Judas Priest singer Rob Halford called it "probably the most evil song ever written" in 2011 on music journalist Bryan Reesman's website. The band chose this as the musical style they wanted to pursue, and now all they needed was the correct name.

They needed only to look at the title of the song they had just written, which fit perfectly. The band dubbed themselves Black Sabbath, and according to guitarist Tony Iommi's 2012 memoir, *Iron Man:*

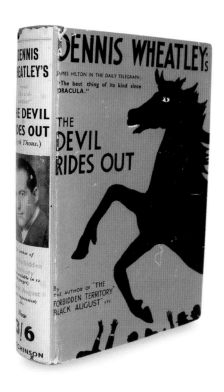

Geezer Butler loved the books of occult novelist Dennis Wheatley. The author (right) appears on a book plate depicting him listening to a satyr go on and on about some bullshit or other.

My Journey through Heaven and Hell with Black Sabbath, they played their first gig under that name in August 1969.

It was good timing—it may have been the same month that the Woodstock Festival had taken place, but it was also the month in which the Manson Family had gone on its murderous spree. Something in the popular culture had shifted, something that had started out innocently enough and was now giving way to something dark and nihilistic. Black Sabbath, the new band with the terrifying sound, was uniquely positioned to comment on it all.

PART 2

BEHIND THE WALL OF SLEEP, 1970–1979

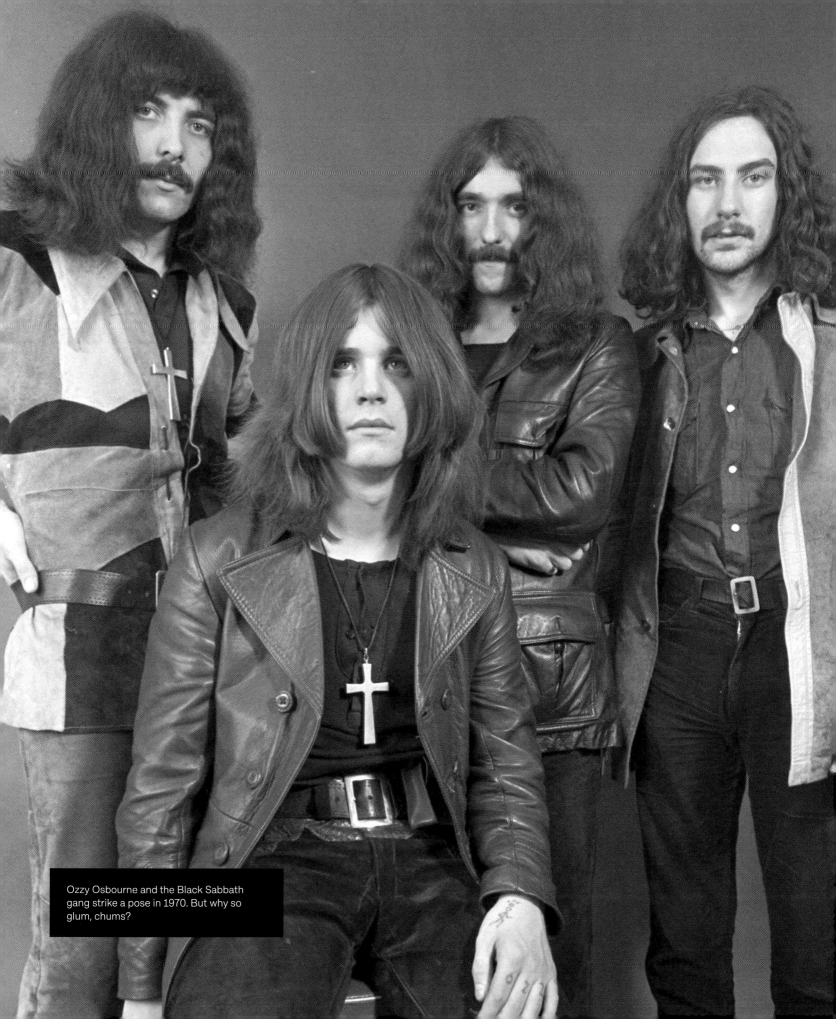

Ozzy Osbourne and the Black Sabbath gang strike a pose in 1970. But why so glum, chums?

06

BLACK SABBATH— *BLACK SABBATH*

THE BAND INVENT A GENRE

FEBRUARY 13, 1970

Nobody was aware of it at the time, but on February 13, 1970—a Friday the 13th, in fact—a momentous event took place. It was the day that the self-titled debut album by Black Sabbath was released in the United Kingdom on Vertigo Records. To this day, the world has never recovered.

One would think that a lot of preparation and planning would have to go into making an album that singlehandedly invented a musical genre, but the opposite was true. According to Osbourne's memoir, the album only took a single day to record, including overdubs.

"Once we'd finished, we spent a couple of hours double-tracking some of the guitar and vocals, and that was that," he wrote. "Done. We were in the pub in time for last orders. It can't have taken any longer than twelve hours in total. That's how albums should be made, in my opinion."

If they didn't spend a lot of time recording, it was partly because they didn't need to. The album basically consisted of their live set, and guitarist Tony Iommi said in his memoir that producer Rodger Bain basically got out of their way and let them do their thing.

"He maybe suggested a couple of things, but the songs were already fairly

structured and sorted," Iommi said. So what you hear on the debut album is an accurate approximation of what the band did live, every night, as a struggling club band.

They did allow themselves one moment of extravagance in the studio. They overdubbed rain and thunder sounds and a tolling bell to the title track, giving it an ominous, funereal atmosphere that's still as effective as ever. But even if they had done without the sound effects, the album would still be a remarkable statement of purpose. Since its release, it's been almost unanimously credited with singlehandedly creating the template for heavy metal.

The album's entire side one is a tour de force. After the title track comes "The Wizard," in which drummer Bill Ward gets to show off his impressive jazz chops, and it's rounded out by "N.I.B." or, if you prefer, "Wasp / Behind the Wall of Sleep / Bassically / N.I.B.," a love song from the point of view of Satan.

Side two is less astonishing. If you scored a U.S. pressing of the album, it opened with "Wicked World," which follows the Sabbath template in pleasingly headbanging fashion, but if you got a U.K. copy instead, it opened with a cover of the Crow song "Evil Woman" which is, in music theory terminology, "not good."

It's followed up by all fourteen minutes of "Sleeping Village" and "Warning," which together come out to about seven minutes of great music and seven minutes of aimless soloing by Iommi. It's not terrible, but it doesn't have nearly the focus and intensity of side one. Iommi may be one of the great rock guitarists of all time, but you will check your watch numerous times before he's done playing the same pentatonic blues runs over and over again.

Ultimately, it doesn't matter. *Black Sabbath* announced Ozzy Osbourne et al.'s arrival on the music scene. While they would go on to make better albums, this was the one that put them on the map. Without it, Ozzy Osbourne the rock star would have just been Ozzy Osbourne the former slaughterhouse employee, who would only have bitten the heads off of bats privately for his own amusement.

The members of Black Sabbath enjoy a local park bench while not being stoned at all.

07

STONEHENGE, WHERE THE DEMONS DWELL

AN INVITATION TO PLAY FOR SOME NEO-DRUIDS

DATE UNKNOWN, 1970

The members of Black Sabbath were suspected of practicing Satanism since their early days, even though it was never true and there is no evidence to support the claim. In fact, early in their career, they were so heavily identified with the occult and Satanism that they were invited by some self-proclaimed Satanists to perform at Stonehenge. According to Ozzy, they received invitations of this kind more than once.

"These freaks with white makeup and black robes would come up to us after our gigs and invite us to black masses at Highgate Cemetery in London," he wrote in his memoir. "I'd say to them, 'Look, mate, the only evil spirits I'm interested in are called whisky, vodka, and gin.'"

Ozzy said that when they received the Stonehenge invitation, they refused. Maybe it was because the Druids built it without any electrical outlets to plug amps into? Whatever the reason, the occultists did not take the news well and said they would curse the band.

It is unknown whether the curse had any effect, but the band were undoubtedly cursed with a reputation as occult practitioners, and their denials did no good. They had students of the occult, witchcraft, and dark magic following them wherever they went. One fateful night on tour, they decided to take decisive action against this state of affairs once and for all.

"We returned to the hotel and found the corridor leading to our rooms completely filled with people wearing black cloaks, sitting on the floor with candles in their hands, chanting, 'Ahhhh,'" Tony Iommi told *Guitar World* in 1992. "So we climbed over them to get to our rooms but could still hear them chanting. . . . So we synchronized our watches, opened our doors at the same time, blew the candles out, and sang 'Happy Birthday' to them."

He also described an incident in which the band found a red cross painted on their dressing room door, which they discovered had been painted in human blood. The person who painted it used his own blood and tried to stab Iommi as he came offstage.

Of course, the group didn't encounter kerfuffles with Satanists alone. They got plenty of grief from Christians too, and matters were not helped when a British nurse committed suicide with a copy of *Paranoid* on her turntable. The band were constantly the subject of ire from the church, and in one case, they succeeded in stopping the band from playing. That one had an unexpected ending, though.

"The Church stopped a few gigs from happening," Iommi said. "A church ran a thing in the papers for weeks before a scheduled performance saying, 'If you let these lads into town, you're committing a sin.' Anyway, they managed to stop us from playing. And the next day the church, for some reason, burned down."

The Black Sabbath dudes take a breather from musically hastening Armageddon by hanging out in front of a mausoleum.

BLACK SABBATH— *PARANOID*

THE BAND'S SECOND ALBUM IS ONE FOR THE AGES

SEPTEMBER 18, 1970

Ozzy holds his gold disc for the *Paranoid* album in one hand and an empty flowerpot in the other, for god knows what reason.

If you're the type of person who would see a book called *Ozzy at 75*, leaf through its contents, and then buy said book, it's probably safe to say you've heard Black Sabbath's 1970 album *Paranoid* before. In fact, even if you can't stand Ozzy Osbourne, you've probably heard it. So why bother going over it again for the millionth time?

It's because it holds up. There may be better-reviewed albums, ones that appeared on more critics' year-end best lists, and others with better production, but *Paranoid* is the one we keep coming back to, despite intimately knowing every one of its grooves. It remains relevant, and listening to it is always rewarding.

While the band's self-titled debut had taken twelve hours to record, they had a little more time to craft a follow-up. Geezer Butler told *Guitar World* in 2004 that they recorded the second album "in about two or three days, live in the studio." *Paranoid* benefits from that bit of extra time, just enough to refine their approach but not so much that it lost any power. It's more focused and contains less screwing around, so the free-form soloing that bogged down a lot of the debut's side two is absent here, thank god.

Side one starts with "War Pigs," a song so monumental that its flaws can be wholly ignored, like the fact that its first lyrics rhyme the word "masses" with "masses." The song comes out swinging, and every note is the right note. And while we kid Geezer Butler for the "masses"/ "masses" *imbroglio*, it's hard to see anything wrong with lyrics like these:

> POLITICIANS HIDE THEMSELVES AWAY,
> THEY ONLY STARTED THE WAR
> WHY SHOULD THEY GO OUT TO FIGHT?
> THEY LEAVE THAT ALL TO THE POOR

These lyrics may have been crafted over fifty years ago, but watching the news for

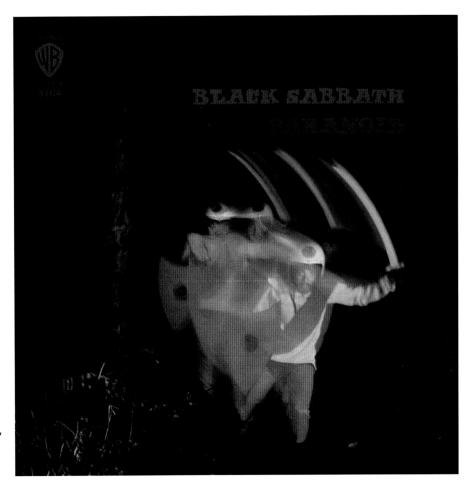

ten seconds shows that they remain as truthful as ever. The same can be said of the title track, which the band have said they threw together from nothing in twenty minutes. Its lyrics perfectly describe the mindset of anyone who feels like shit and can't get out from under it. It's impossible not to see unvarnished truth in them.

After the mellow interlude of "Planet Caravan" comes "Iron Man," whose main riff deserves mention on the same guitar store signs that forbid the playing of "Smoke on the Water." The whole point of the song is that riff, with Ozzy's nasal voice stacked on top of it, doubling the chord progression for maximum ham-handedness. It also doesn't suck that the iconic opening statement, "I am Iron Man," was spoken into a fan, an activity that has brought hours of excitement to the young and the young at heart for decades.

Side two lacks a clear anthem like those found on side one, but it still engages. "Electric Funeral," "Hand of Doom," and "Fairies Wear Boots" show the band perfectly balancing gloomy riffs with the mighty swing of drummer Bill Ward, something no Sabbath clone band has ever managed to get right, and never will. It's too distinct and too specific to those four guys, and none of their 1970s hard rock contemporaries ever managed to crack the code.

Black Sabbath would make more musically accomplished albums, and Ozzy Osbourne would make records that charted higher. Be that as it may, *Paranoid* is a towering achievement, and Ozzy, Tony, Geezer, and Bill will forever live in its shadow.

A bespectacled Ozzy Osbourne wows his bandmates with a faithful interpretation of John Cage's *4' 33"*.

09

FIRST MARRIAGE BLUES

DATE UNKNOWN, 1971

While Ozzy Osbourne's marriage to his manager Sharon is known to anyone who follows the gossip rags, she's not his first spouse. That prize goes to one Thelma Riley, known today as Thelma Mayfair, and at one point, Thelma Osbourne.

Osbourne's first family has pretty much stayed out of the spotlight. Indeed, many people didn't even know they existed until they saw the 2011 documentary *God Bless Ozzy Osbourne*. But exist they do, even if they never had a reality show made about them.

According to the memoir *I Am Ozzy*, the singer met his first wife in 1971 at a Birmingham nightclub called the Rum Runner, where she was an employee. As befits a young couple with their whole lives ahead of them, they married that

same year and eventually had two children. The singer even adopted Thelma's first son, Elliot, something you don't do unless you think your marriage will last.

It didn't. The singer called the marriage a "terrible mistake" in the documentary *God Bless Ozzy Osbourne*, which features an all-time cringe moment when he confesses that he doesn't even remember when his children with Thelma were born.

"Shortly after I became successful with Black Sabbath, I met Thelma in a nightclub," he said. "Then we got married, and we had two children, Jessica and Louis. We bought a house for 20,000 pounds, I thought, 'I have arrived.' Not realizing it was a giant mirage. Something ain't feeling right."

The "something" that wasn't feeling right may have been that his fondness for drugs and alcohol, combined with living the life of a touring musician, made being a father in the conventional sense close to impossible. In *God Bless Ozzy Osbourne*, his son Louis said that the singer's crimes were mainly sins of omission—in other words, he wasn't around much, and when he was, he was drunk.

"When he was around, and he wasn't pissed, he was a great father," Louis said. "But that was kind of seldom, really. I just have a lot of memories of him being drunk, random shit like driving cars across fields and crashing them in the middle of the night, and stuff like that. It's not good for family life, really."

Louis added that the only thing he ever really wanted was for his famous dad to remember his birthday, but that was a bridge too far.

"It was all I wanted, but he just couldn't remember that," he said.

Ozzy himself co-signed on Louis's version of events. He said that he had believed that having rock star money would make everything in his family's life go smoothly, but that same rock star money would get spent on the drugs and alcohol that made him an absentee father, even when he was at home. Ultimately, he and Thelma divorced in 1982, and Osbourne took full responsibility for all of it.

"I behaved fucking badly," he admitted. "The way I treated Thelma, it was wrong. I treated her really badly and the kids, two children. I was a very selfish, self-centered, egotistical guy, and I fucked around from day one, and that ain't cool. And my wife just had enough."

Ozzy in 1978 with Louis and Jessica Osbourne, his two children from his first marriage. The union sadly didn't work out, for which Ozzy took full responsibility.

10

BLACK SABBATH— *MASTER OF REALITY*

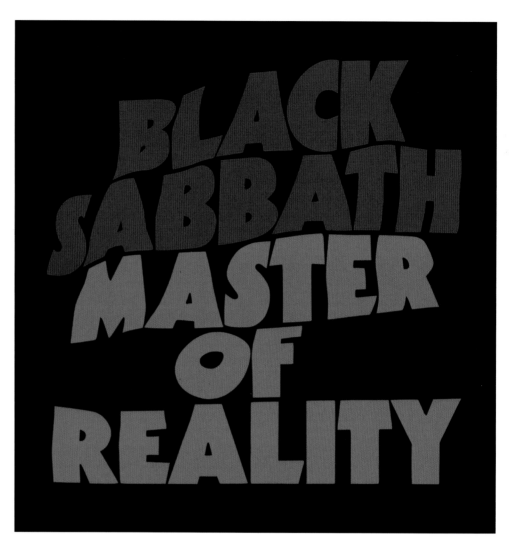

THE BAND'S THIRD ALBUM IS THEIR HEAVIEST EVER

JULY 21, 1971

The third Black Sabbath album, *Master of Reality*, was released in 1971. Rodger Bain, who had produced the first two albums, came back to perform production services on this one. While many bands famously suffer from creative constipation when making "the difficult third album," Sabbath had no such issues.

If Black Sabbath can be said to have a first era, *Master of Reality* is the perfect coda to it. That era was marked mainly by bludgeoning riffs and primitive drumming, and on this album, the band pull no punches in those areas. It opens with the stoner anthem "Sweet Leaf," which follows a template similar to the one used for "Iron Man"—monstrously heavy riff, monstrously heavy riff again, faster

mid-section with lots of soloing, and then back to the monstrously heavy riff.

Except for "Solitude" on side two and the brief acoustic interludes "Embryo" and "Orchid," the mission statement of this album is heaviness at any cost, even if that cost is the production. The bass seems louder in the mix than the guitar, giving the album monstrous weight that doesn't let up. The members of Metallica should have been forced to listen to this record before foisting the deeply frustrating, bass-free mix of their 1988 album ... *And Justice for All* onto an unsuspecting public.

The second song, "After Forever," is more upbeat. While the band have been accused of practicing Satanism since its inception, the lyrics are unabashedly pro-Christian. It contains such couplets as "I've seen the light and I've changed my ways" and "God is the only way to love," phrases that appear nowhere in *The Satanic Bible*.

Things get really menacing with the side one closer, "Children of the Grave." Built on a chugging riff in shuffle time that

would turn up a decade later on Blondie's "Call Me," the song describes the hope that a future generation might stop the world from committing nuclear suicide. It's a case of music and subject matter playing perfectly off of one another, a la chocolate and peanut butter.

After the brief acoustic breather "Orchid," side two starts in earnest with "Lord

of This World," another selection that's more Christian than a lot of the band's detractors would like to admit. Like the songs on side one, it's heavy as fuck, but it has a status as album filler simply because there's so much other good stuff here. If it had appeared on *Technical Ecstasy* or *13*, it would have been the best song on those albums, but sadly here it gets slightly overshadowed by all the competition, which is pretty stiff.

The album closes with "Into the Void." Opening with a slow, chromatic, and discordant riff, it makes its leisurely way to the main section of the song, a midtempo plodder about people escaping a polluted planet Earth in the hopes of finding a new start. While it's unlikely that the song inspired *Wall-E*, it's interesting to note that Black Sabbath were singing about this type of stuff when almost no one else was. Zager and Evans might have been worried about the year 2525, but in the year of our lord 1971, Black Sabbath used their heaviest record yet to let us know it was already too late.

It would be wrong to say that Black Sabbath "sold out" after this record, but it caps a run of three albums that formed the foundation for heavy metal, and the band would become creatively restless afterward. Having said that, *Master of Reality* shows the band firing on all cylinders and working as a team toward a common goal, which sadly would become less and less the case as time went on.

Ozzy does his best Richard Nixon impersonation in an undisclosed location in 1971.

11

IS THERE A DOCTOR IN THE TEA SHOP?

BABIES ARE BORN IN THE DARNEDEST PLACES

Ozzy's first wife, Thelma, flanked by their daughter Jessica (left), their son Louis (seated), and Thelma's son Elliot (right) in 1976. By his own admission, he was never around much, so Ozzy's absence from this photo is fitting.

While Ozzy Osbourne's first marriage may not have worked out, it still had moments that are amusing in retrospect, particularly after several decades, and especially if none of it happened to you or any of your loved ones. Such a moment was detailed in *I Am Ozzy*, in which the singer recounted the joyous day that his first daughter, Jessica, was born.

Osbourne recounts how, early in Black Sabbath's career, all of his rock star dreams seemed to be coming true. He wasn't seeing any actual money (more on that later), but in those early days, anything he needed was just one phone call away, and that call went to the band's manager, Patrick Meehan.

On this occasion, the thing that he needed was a house. Thelma was pregnant, and the tiny apartment they were living in would not provide enough room for the growing family. After a lot of house-hunting, they decided on one in Staffordshire with four bedrooms, a sauna, a studio, and lots of land.

The happy couple with dreams of the future was in a tea shop in Worcestershire when they made the decision. Suddenly, Thelma asked Ozzy if he could hear "that clicking noise."

He could, but it took a moment to identify where it was coming from.

"I looked down and saw a big puddle under Thelma's chair," he wrote. "Something was dripping from under her dress."

Thelma informed him that her water had broken, and she was about to experience the miracle of childbirth. She asked him to drive her to the hospital, and he said that he couldn't since he didn't have a driver's license. Furthermore, he was drunk. She made the quite valid points that nothing had ever stopped him from breaking the law before and that he had

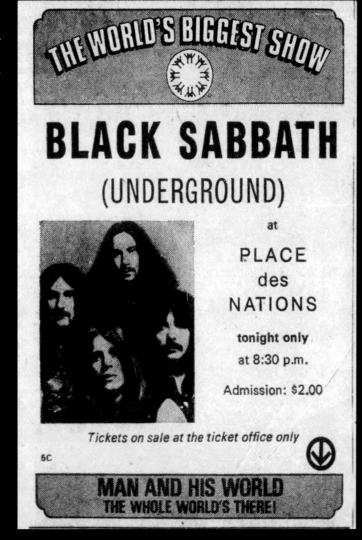

been "drunk since 1967," so he was just going to have to cross his fingers and hope for the best.

He wrote that it took about twenty minutes just to get Thelma's car moving. As he struggled, she gave him instructions on all the most rudimentary aspects of operating a motor vehicle, including putting his foot on the gas pedal. She did so as she moaned and groaned her way through the contractions, begging her husband to go faster.

They defied the odds and made it to Queen Elizabeth Hospital in Edgbaston. Osbourne described it as miraculous that they didn't plow into the back of an

ambulance. At 11:20 that night, Jessica Osbourne came into the world. Inspired by the glittery constellations in the January sky, she was given the middle name Starshine.

Today, the singer has no shortage of stories about things he did while he was drunk, but this was the only time his activity while inebriated was driving someone to a hospital to have a baby. Still, he should be commended for keeping his wits about him and not killing anybody, and for avoiding the headline that he feared he would see in the newspaper—"ROCKER'S TOT IN FREAK M-WAY TRAGEDY."

12

SNIFF, SNIFF, SNORT

RECORDING *VOL. 4* IS FUELED BY COCAINE

MAY 1972

Black Sabbath's 1972 album *Vol. 4* is considered one of the group's finest slabs of vinyl, and who could argue? It's the sound of a band coming into their own.

"It's the first album we've produced ourselves," Ozzy Osbourne told *Sounds* upon the album's release. "I think we're all very happy."

Geezer Butler told the *Guardian* in 2013 that the album had cost $60,000 to record, which in 1972 dollars translates to approximately $400,000 today, a fraction of what a lot of other rockers would spend to make their own records. Metallica spent over $1 million on their self-titled 1991 album, whose massive riffs and slow tempos owe more than just a passing debt to the Birmingham foursome, and that amount is not even indexed for inflation. So the guys in Sabbath deserve credit for keeping studio costs low on their first self-produced effort. Kudos!

Where it all went screwy was when it came to the cocaine budget. It was the 1970s, the drug was very much in vogue, and it certainly made more than one appearance at recording studios during the Me Decade. However, Black Sabbath managed the neat trick of spending more money on disco dust than they spent recording the actual album.

Butler said that between the first session and the last, the group spent $75,000 on cocaine. For people who like to play with calculators, that means the cocaine budget exceeded the recording budget by 25 percent and would translate to almost $500,000 when adjusted for inflation. But while Osbourne is the Sabbath alumnus with the most extensive reputation for drug intake, Tony Iommi told the *Guardian* that the singer was not alone in his alarming consumption rate.

"I was doing coke left, right and center, and quaaludes, and God knows what else," he said.

He also added that the cocaine made them very popular with other musicians. However, that popularity was 100 percent opportunistic, self-serving, and phony.

"That's why we used to have all the musicians turning up at our house at

the time, pretending they're coming to visit us," Iommi told *Rolling Stone*.

He said that the cocaine was flown in by private plane. So much of it was being ingested that the band initially intended to call the album *Snowblind*. Sadly, the record company would have none of it, and they were forced to change the title to *Vol. 4*.

Oh, well. "Snowblind," the track, still remains, and that song effectively explains in under six minutes what the band was going through at the time. For all the powder they were putting up their noses, the lyrics would seem to suggest that no one in the band was actually having a good time, and they already knew that contrary to what drummer Sam McPherson said in *Walk Hard: The Dewey Cox Story*, it would not turn all their bad feelings into good feelings.

Ozzy in 1971, making sure his plastic spoon still smells fresh.

13

BLACK SABBATH—
VOL. 4

THE BAND'S FOURTH ALBUM IS A FAN FAVORITE

SEPTEMBER 25, 1972

Ozzy and the Sabs decimate London's Royal Albert Hall in 1972, leaving only a smoldering crater in their wake.

Master of Reality may have been the closing salvo of the first era of Black Sabbath, but the next one started with an album that many consider the best thing the group ever recorded. Titled *Vol. 4*, it was released in 1972 and showed the band straddling the line between their early, primitive brutality and something a little more sophisticated. Not so sophisticated that it dulled the album's edge, mind you, but sophisticated enough to let fans know the band were trying new things.

The album opens with "Wheels of Confusion," whose eight-minute, epic structure provided a template for songs that would appear on later albums, such as "The Thrill of It All" and "The Writ" from 1975's *Sabotage*. After the midtempo "Tomorrow's Dream" comes "Changes," a song with no precedent in the Black Sabbath catalog.

"Changes" is a piano ballad with some Mellotron over the top of it. Apart from those instruments and Ozzy's voice, that's about it. It was composed by Iommi, who didn't even play the piano but could manipulate it well enough to coax a song out of it. Butler's lyrics, which were inspired by the collapse of Bill Ward's first marriage, are as simple as it gets, but they serve the song well. Just like they did with the song "Paranoid," the band had the insight to know when they were onto something, and they should get out of its way and let it happen.

Over thirty years later, in 2003, Ozzy would re-record the song, this time as a duet with his daughter Kelly. It topped the UK singles chart and sold one million copies, while at the same time landing at #27 in the *Village Voice's* ranking of the "50 Worst Songs of the '00s."

The side ends with "Supernaut" and is followed on the next by "Snowblind." The band had collectively gone head over heels for cocaine, consuming it in superhuman amounts, but if the song

is any indication, they were feeling conflicted about it at the same time. The lyrics alternate between stubborn endorsement of the drug and what sounds like an understanding that keeping it up could lead to nothing good. The mid-section even contains some lyrics that sound like an intervention gone wrong.

DON'T YOU THINK I KNOW WHAT I'M DOING, DON'T TELL ME THAT IT'S DOING ME WRONG YOU'RE THE ONE WHO'S REALLY THE LOSER, THIS IS WHERE I FEEL I BELONG

All that's missing is "I can stop any time I want." It's followed by "Cornucopia," a song whose structure and time changes proved highly challenging to Bill Ward. By his own account, he kept fucking it up during the recording, leading him to believe he would be fired from the band. After the acoustic guitar piece "Laguna Sunrise" and the throwaway "St. Vitus Dance," the album wraps up with "Under the Sun," whose massive opening section is easily one of the heaviest things the band ever recorded. When it reaches its coda, it slows down and slows down and slows down agonizingly, until the end of the song almost feels like a relief.

Vol. 4 was the most diverse record yet in the Sabbath catalog, and it planted some

seeds that would bear fruit on subsequent albums. It was also in some ways the first indication that all was not well within the band—their drug use was accelerating, and while they were still able to keep it together well enough to tour, record, and perform their duties as the world's premier sludge purveyors, that would get to be less and less the case in the coming years. But as a standalone achievement, it's very impressive, and in his memoir, the singer said it was "one of Black Sabbath's best-ever albums."

14

I GOT IT FROM AGNES, SHE GOT IT FROM JIM

TREATING GONORRHEA THE OZZY WAY

DATE UNKNOWN, 1972

Rock musicians in the 1970s had a plum gig for a little while there. Women had just started using the birth control pill, and AIDS wouldn't rear its head until the next decade, so rockers could travel the globe and have lots and lots of unprotected sex with no consequences but for the occasional, non-fatal, sexually transmitted disease.

Treating an STD that had planted a flag in a particular rock star penis was a relatively simple thing. Said rock star would go to the doctor and get a shot of penicillin, clearing it right up. This allowed said rock star to go home to his wife and make church-sanctioned love within the sacrament of marriage, free from concern that he would pass along some ill-intentioned virus or bacterium.

In his memoir, Ozzy said he had already learned of the curative powers of penicillin "after getting the clap one time" and shared his knowledge with Tony, Geezer, and some of the road crew. It was after the making of *Vol. 4*, they had played some shows, and they had known some groupies in the biblical sense. This led them to become living incarnations of the Frank Zappa song "Why Does It Hurt When I Pee?"

The singer and his coterie made their way to the emergency room for what he called a "safety shot." When they all arrived at the emergency room, none of them could work up the courage to check themselves in and say why they were there. They wanted Ozzy to do it, and not just because it wasn't his first time trying to ward off gonorrhea.

"No one had the bottle to tell the good-looking chick on the front desk why we were there," he wrote. "So they were all going, 'Go on, Ozzy, you tell her, you don't care, you're fucking crazy, you are.'"

Despite his reputation as a wild man, Ozzy did not take to the request with much enthusiasm. He said that when he reached the front desk, he was too embarrassed to give the real reason why he and his traveling companions were all there, so he said he had broken his ribs. As the other people in his party checked themselves in, they would say, "I've got what he's got" and point at him. Apparently, they had all broken their ribs at the same time. Remarkable!

Osbourne recalled that eventually, someone in his group must have copped to the actual problem. He was led into

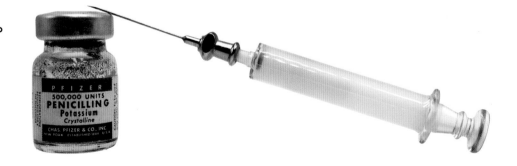

a room by "this bloke in a white suit," and in that room, he was greeted by the sight of Tony, Geezer, and a few other hirsute Englishmen, "all bent over with their trousers down, their lily-white arses ready for their penicillin jabs."

While the singer did not know which member of their party finally relented and told the doctors what they needed to know, that man should be singled out for his candor. Furthermore, he should be thanked for the fact that after the tour ended, everyone's wives didn't find out what their husbands had been up to by having their most personal areas turn into monsters from 1982's *The Thing*.

Ozzy in Amsterdam in 1971, explaining how politicians hide themselves away.

15

"SUCH A DREADFUL FLU"

THE VICAR, THE ROCKER, HIS WIFE, AND THE HASH CAKE

DATE UNKNOWN, 1973

Ah, edibles. In this day and age, it's easy to have just the right amount, but in the 1970s, it was more of a crapshoot. If you baked some hash into a cake—for example—you couldn't really predict what kind of an effect it would have. It was entirely possible to go from "This is delicious cake" to "Please drive me to the emergency room" in the space of an hour.

Ozzy told *GQ* that he had bought some hash and baked a cake with it at one point during his doomed first marriage. He told his then-wife Thelma not to eat it or let anyone else eat it, saying only that "It will be bad." Then he went off to the pub and, Ozzy being Ozzy, was gone for "a few days."

When he finally turned up at home again after his bender, he was greeted by the sight of his wife and the local vicar, whom she was entertaining in their home. Thelma had apparently forgotten her husband's dire warning and given the vicar a cup of tea with a slice of the "bad" cake. It had an overpowering effect on the clergyman, who was slumped over and unconscious in their kitchen. Ozzy, who didn't have a driver's license (still!), decided to do the decent thing and take the vicar home in his car.

"I had to drag him out by his hair, push him in the back of his car, drive him to his door and then walk home," the singer told *GQ*. Ozzy didn't see the vicar for two weeks, and during that time, he worried that his cake might have actually killed the guy. Luckily, he ran into the man of the cloth in a pub, and the man was none the wiser about what had happened.

"I must have caught such a dreadful flu at yours," the vicar told him. "I hallucinated for three days and had to miss church."

Tim Jones, the journalist conducting the interview for *GQ*, said what many of us are thinking: The most surprising thing to him about the story was that Osbourne had a vicar in his home in the first place. The singer said that this was typical when you moved to rural England.

"When you move into the countryside, they try to get you into the congregation and welcome you to the community," he explained. "They invite you for a chat, see if you want to confess a few things."

Jones asked if that sounded appealing to Osbourne, whose answer was predictably dismissive.

"If I'd have gone, I'd still be there now, fucking confessing all my sins!"

Ozzy in a rare moment of quiet reflection in 1973. Perhaps he was thinking, "In eight years, what kind of bird should I decapitate?"

Black Sabbath hitting their stride onstage, before substances, egos, and the music business got in the way.

16

BLACK SABBATH— *SABBATH BLOODY SABBATH*

THE BAND GOES PROG ROCK

DECEMBER 1, 1973

The fifth Black Sabbath album, *Sabbath Bloody Sabbath*, was released in 1973. In contrast to the albums they had recorded previously, this one was a much heavier lift. The days of recording an entire album in one day and mixing it the next were over, and not just because there was more money to pay for studio time. Instead, drugs and fatigue conspired to gum up the works.

The band had just completed touring to support *Vol. 4*, and that jaunt saw the band at their most coked-up yet. It culminated in a tour date at the Hollywood Bowl that ended in an ignominious fashion.

"Tony had been doing coke literally for days—we all had, but Tony had gone over the edge," Osbourne wrote in *I Am Ozzy*. "I mean, that stuff just twists your whole idea of reality. You start seeing things that aren't there. And Tony was *gone*. Near the end of the gig, he walked off stage and collapsed."

The band returned to Los Angeles to record the follow-up to *Vol. 4*, but they were too drained from drugs and touring to come up with new material. They returned to the UK and started again at a castle in Gloucestershire, and the dark, gloomy surroundings inspired them. They were writing again, and they produced some anthems worthy of the Black Sabbath name.

The album kicks off grandly with the title track, which boasts two of the greatest riffs the band ever recorded—the main

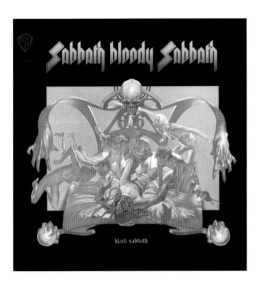

one and the "Where can you run to?" riff that only Black Sabbath could possibly produce. It's followed by "A National Acrobat," which is utterly brilliant until the end section, which seems surgically grafted on from some other song.

After the acoustic guitar interlude appropriately named "Fluff" comes the mighty "Sabbra Cadabra," a song that wisely keeps it simple structure-wise and is one of the band's greatest deep cuts. It also features contributions from keyboard player Rick Wakeman, who happened to be in the same studio recording with

Yes. According to Tony Iommi's memoir, Wakeman was compensated for his services entirely in beer.

Side two opens with "Killing Yourself to Live," another masterpiece of a deep cut, which is followed by "Who Are You?" This is one of the worst songs the original band ever recorded. Sorry. The album ends with "Looking for Today" and "Spiral Architect," two songs that are pretty solid but provide additional evidence for Ozzy's claim that things were starting to go south within the band, both as a unit and for him personally.

"*Sabbath Bloody Sabbath* was really the album after which I should have said goodbye because, after that, I really started unraveling," he wrote in his memoir. "Then we ended up falling out of favor with each other."

Despite all the trouble behind the scenes, *Sabbath Bloody Sabbath* still holds up, provided you skip "Fluff" and "Who Are You." At the time of its release, it was the first Sabbath album to get a good review from *Rolling Stone*, and the band members themselves have said favorable things about it in retrospect, including Ozzy.

"[*Sabbath Bloody Sabbath* was] our last truly great album," he wrote in his memoir. "With the music, we'd managed to strike just the right balance between our old heaviness and our new, 'experimental' side."

Black Sabbath on the concert stage. The date and venue may be unknown, but the fact that the Sabs left nothing but devastation in their wake is *known*.

BLACK SABBATH— *SABOTAGE*

THE MUSIC BUSINESS STARTS TO INTRUDE

JULY 28, 1975

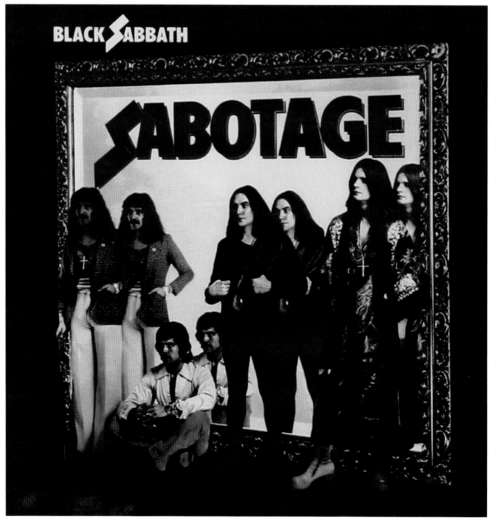

By the time Black Sabbath released their sixth album, 1975's *Sabotage*, the band had become a very different entity than it had been just a few years before. The Black Sabbath that had come up in nightclubs was a tightly knit unit working toward a common creative goal. By the middle of the decade, they were fracturing, and the cohesion that had marked their first era was a thing of the past. One of the stressors was the band's decision to fire their manager, Patrick Meehan.

"Patrick Meehan never gave you a straight answer when you asked him how much dough you were making," Osbourne said. It led the band to suspect that they were being cheated out of money that had been coming to them, prompting the firing.

Meehan responded by taking legal action against the band, plunging them into a period that bassist Geezer Butler described in *Louder Sound* as "total chaos."

The chaos Butler described led to the band taking almost a year to finish recording *Sabotage*, a clear sign that the common cause and camaraderie among the band that had made them able to record their debut in twelve hours was gone. The ongoing intake of drugs and alcohol didn't help.

Despite all the *agita* and *tsuris* surrounding the band at this time, *Sabotage* still has some great moments, some of which are worthy to stand shoulder to shoulder with their best work.

The album opener "Hole in the Sky" is a straight banger, as the kids say, based around a guitar riff that takes no prisoners. Iommi explained that if the guitars were a bit grittier-sounding than they had been on *Sabbath Bloody Sabbath*, it was because he was channeling all of his rage over the lawsuit into his guitar tone.

After the acoustic guitar instrumental "Don't Start (Too Late)" comes "Symptom of the Universe," whose first section is based around a riff that predates the thrash metal bands of the next decade. Surprisingly, the song transitions into a more delicate section full of acoustic guitars and Ozzy singing lyrics about the "summer skies of love." It works a lot better than it should.

Side one is rounded out by the almost ten-minute "Megalomania," which contains a bunch of great riffs and an excellent vocal performance by Osbourne. Unfortunately, it's a little scattered and overstays its welcome by several minutes. This pattern sadly repeats itself throughout the record. Side two's "Thrill of It All" and "The Writ" both start out with a minute or two of absolutely stone-cold classic Sabbath crunch, which then gets abandoned in favor of several minutes of twee, overly ornate music that just doesn't connect.

It's a shame because those songs in simplified form could have been classics, but stylistically the band seem impatient with just riding the riff and wanders from overelaborate structure to overelaborate structure. If you imagine the song "Iron Man" with the main riff being played once, followed by six minutes of imitation-prog foolishness, then that's the effect these songs have.

While much of *Sabotage* sounds like a band that's running out of gas, enough of it is at a sufficiently pleasing level that it's considered one of the band's classic albums, even if it doesn't inspire the same level of enthusiasm as a record like *Paranoid*. And according to Iommi, the song "Am I Going Insane (Radio)" pointed toward the future for at least one of them.

"In hindsight, it was kind of a precursor for [Ozzy's] solo career," he told *Louder Sound*. "His personality was blooming on this song."

Slay! Batter! Punish! Black Sabbath deluges Holland in heavy metal magma in 1975.

18

"BITS OF BEAK"

OZZY GOES ON A DRUNKEN POULTRY RAMPAGE

DATE UNKNOWN, 1976

God bless that Thelma Riley Osbourne Mayfair. She tried her darnedest to turn her husband Ozzy into something resembling a typical human husband, but the odds were just not on her side. Love does not conquer all, even if you try to smooth the way by keeping live chickens at your home as a way of reinforcing its status as a pastoral country manor.

Ozzy said in his memoir that Thelma kept a bunch of chickens in a coop at their home and would task her famous husband with feeding them. So far, so good. Unfortunately, one mid-1970s evening around sunset, Thelma asked her husband to feed the chickens. He was very preoccupied with problems that were beginning to arise for the group, such as a tax bill for $1 million and a need for a new musical direction on the part of other band members. By his own recollection, all the pressure was too much for him, and between that and the Scotch he had been drinking, he snapped. He brought a shotgun to the chicken coop.

"Anyone laid any eggs?" he asked. When he didn't get a response because they were chickens and didn't speak English, he informed them of their fate. "Too bad."

Osbourne clicked the safety off and began executing the chickens one by one.

"The sound of the gun was fucking deafening, and it echoed across the fields for what seemed like miles in all directions," he wrote. "And with every shot, there was a white flash that lit up the coop and the garden around it, followed by a strong whiff of gun-powder. I was feeling much better now."

He may have felt better, but any unsuspecting onlookers would have been horrified to see the aftermath of his poultry holocaust.

"By the time I was done, there was blood and feathers and bits of beak all over the fucking place," he said. "It looked as though someone had thrown a bucket of chicken guts at me and then emptied a pillow over my head. . . . But I felt fucking fabulous—like someone had just lifted a three-ton anvil off my back."

As if that wasn't enough carnage and horror, Osbourne emptied a can full of gasoline all over the crime scene and flicked a lit cigarette into the coop. It was instantly engulfed in flames, and he began

Ozzy outside his home in 1978. Despite the smile on his face, there was trouble in paradise, and he and Black Sabbath would part ways a year later.

tossing unused shotgun cartridges into the conflagration. As they began to pop, he noticed that one chicken had escaped, and he started chasing it, for reasons best known to him.

"I didn't know what the fuck was wrong with me, or why I was doing what I was doing," he wrote in his memoir. "All I knew was that I was possessed with this insane, uncontrollable rage at all chickenkind."

As he chased the lone survivor chicken, an elderly neighbor was roused from her home by all the commotion. She came out with a garden hoe, and she was greeted by a drunk, coked-up Osbourne, clad only in a bathrobe and "welly" boots. She said to him the only thing that there really was to say upon seeing such a thing.

"'Ah, good evening, Mr. Osbourne,'" she said. "'I see you're back from America.'"

19

BLACK SABBATH—*TECHNICAL ECSTASY*

THE HMS *SABBATH* HITS A STYLISTIC ICEBERG

SEPTEMBER 25, 1976

Ozzy in 1976, showing us all that if we open our hearts and believe in ourselves, the smiles will be contagious.

Oy, this one.

While the band members' opinions vary as to which Black Sabbath album constitutes the official moment of shark-jumping, many fans are united in their assessment of where it all went wrong. The plethora of unlicensed fan merchandise that says "You can only trust the first six Black Sabbath albums" should give you a clue. Many believe the band lost the plot on their 1976 album *Technical Ecstasy*, and they may have a point.

First, the good news—*Technical Ecstasy* has some good moments, and those moments comprise about 40 percent of the album.

That's it. That's the good news.

Unfortunately, there's no one song on the entire thing that's good all the way through, and it makes for a very frustrating listen. If the band had taken the parts that really work and developed those into complete songs, it could have been a contender. Unfortunately, the syndrome that the band acquired on *Sabotage*, which could be politely described as "grafting random riffs and beats together," had advanced significantly since the previous album, making each song a Frankenstein's monster, with unrelated limbs and sinew all sewn together.

BLACK SABBATH

TECHNICAL ECSTASY

It's tempting to blame the emergence of punk rock for this state of affairs, as many bands of Sabbath's vintage famously found themselves struggling to compete with the new sound. In his 2013 book *Black Sabbath: Symptom of the Universe*, author Mick Wall disagreed, blaming the burgeoning soft rock movement, which had made million-sellers out of bands like Fleetwood Mac. In Wall's opinion, Tony Iommi was trying to chase that sound and somehow make it fit the Black Sabbath mold, a fool's errand.

"To try and force that sound on Black Sabbath was like trying to put lamb's wool on a suit of armor," he wrote. "It just didn't work, pleasing nobody."

As for the music itself, the rockers that fare the best are "You Won't Change Me," "All Moving Parts (Stand Still)," and "Dirty Women." That last one was actually resurrected for the band's 2013 reunion tour, a surprise appearance in the set whose seven-minute running time offered concertgoers a perfect opportunity to go to the bathroom.

Shockingly, the music that fares the best on *Technical Ecstasy* belongs to its two ballads, "It's Alright" and "She's Gone." Bill Ward wrote and sang "It's Alright,"

which owes more than a passing resemblance to Paul McCartney's "Maybe I'm Amazed," particularly during the guitar solo.

The song "Rock 'n' Roll Doctor," which appears on side two, is meanwhile the worst in the Black Sabbath catalog up to that point. A completely phoned-in mediocrity that overstays its welcome even at three and a half minutes, it contains almost every hard rock cliché you can think of, a shocking fate for a band who less than a decade before had pioneered a brand-new sound, unlike anything that had come before. If you wanted to argue that Black Sabbath should have broken up after *Sabotage*, "Rock 'n' Roll Doctor" is the horrible, terrible, very bad, no-good song that would be exhibit A.

Ozzy left the band for the first time after completing the world tour, and though he would return for one more album, the situation was in too advanced a state of rot to be improved. In the meantime, attempts have been made to rehabilitate this much-maligned album, and in 2021 Porcupine Tree's Steven Wilson remixed it for a commemorative box set.

Fun Fact: In 2014, Geezer Butler told *Uncut* that they recorded *Technical Ecstasy* right after the Eagles had recorded *Hotel California* in the same studio. "Before we could start recording, we had to scrape all the cocaine out of the mixing board," he said. "I think they'd left about a pound of cocaine in the board."

BLACK SABBATH with **WISHBONE ASH**

DANIEL SIMMONDS

Thursday **March 2nd** **7:30**

Miami Beach Convention Hall

Ticket $4.50, 5

ALL SEATS RES

TICKETS AVAILABLE
RECORD WORLD

MILE CO - CASABLANCA - RECORD BAR
MIAMI - MIAMI DADE JUNIOR
GRAND CENTRAL STATION - CORAL GABLE

Black Sabbath

with

MAHOGONY RUSH

SEATTLE ARENA
7:30 PM · SEPTEMBER 12

Tickets Available at Fidelity Lane Shoreline Music Bell Book & Candle (Bellevue)
Campus Music Lamonts (Burien) Bon Marche (Tacoma Only) Carousell Music (Everett)
present by the John Bauer Concert Co.

Tuesday, February 15, 7:30pm

IN FORT WAYNE

CELEBRATION
PRODUCTIONS

IS VERY PROUD TO PRESENT

'Black Sabbath'

WITH SPECIAL GUEST

JOURNEY
and TARGET

MEMORIAL COLISEUM

$6.50 in advance $7 day of show

Edward R. Panian   Graphics Design

TICKET OUTLETS
Coliseum box office
Slatewood records
Nickelodeon's (Marion, Wabash)
Mind Dust Music (Elida, Ohio)
Butterfly records (Warsaw)
Suspended Cord (Elkhart)
Just for the records (Mishawaka)
Boogie records (Mishawaka)
Record Joint (Niles)

STARLITE FESTIVAL

BLACK SABBATH

LYNYRD SKYNYRD

SPECIAL GUEST

PETER FRAMPTON

DAY SEPTEMBER 5   5 PM-11 PM.
ORANGE SHOW STADIUM
SAN BERNARDINO

$6.50 available at all Liberty & Mutual Agencies, Muntz Stereo, Gillette
Arcade) in Riverside, all Ticketron Locations and at the Orange Show
Ticket Agency. For information call (714) 86

PACIFIC PRESENTA

20

BLACK SABBATH— *NEVER SAY DIE!*

OZZY AND SABBATH GO ONE MORE ROUND

SEPTEMBER 28, 1978

Ozzy waves hello to the good people at Detroit's Cobo Arena in 1978.

1978's *Never Say Die!* was the eighth studio album by Black Sabbath in as many years, and it marked the last album Ozzy Osbourne would make with the band until 2013's *13*. Like *Technical Ecstasy*, the album suffers from trying to go in too many directions at once, and about half of those directions should have been rejected. Unfortunately, circumstances didn't allow for a considered approach.

Ozzy had left Black Sabbath briefly after *Technical Ecstasy*, and he was replaced with Savoy Brown's Dave Walker. It was the shortest of unions, but the band had written some new material with him in that time. According to Tony Iommi's memoir, Osbourne came back to the band soon after but flatly refused to do any of the songs they had written with Walker. This put the band in the position of writing a song from scratch in the daytime and recording it that night.

"We never had time to review the tracks and make changes," Iommi told *Guitar World* in 1992. "As a result, the album sounds very confused."

While Iommi has a point, *Never Say Die!* is a more successful album than its predecessor. The title track opens the album as energetically as anyone could ask for and keeps the song's structure straightforward. No unnecessary detours into textures lifted from Electric Light Orchestra albums here. Side one ends with "A Hard Road," which gets a little long in the tooth at six minutes but overall is a straightforward and enjoyable song.

The rest of the record is full of half-realized ideas, which makes sense given Iommi's recollection of the circumstances behind it. In the case of the instrumental, "Breakout," one wonders why they even bothered at all, and on the album closer, "Swinging the Chain," Bill Ward provides lead vocals because Osbourne refused to do so. The disharmony in the group was starting to show up in the finished product.

Never Say Die! is a tragic album for several reasons, not the least of which is the time constraints involved in making it. If it had been allowed to evolve naturally, it's entirely possible that the good ideas would have risen to the top and been worked up into good songs. Sadder still is the fact that this album is the sound of four guys who had come up together and triumphed together and who now couldn't find the inspiration that had once united them. It goes out with neither a bang nor with a whimper, but with an "I don't know . . . Maybe the next album will be better?"

Today, it's hard to tell if the bad atmosphere surrounding *Never Say Die!* reflected the band's constant drug use, creative restlessness, or personal animus.

But we do know that Ozzy Osbourne is decidedly not a fan, as he made clear in an interview with *After Hours* in 1981.

"The last album I did with Sabbath was *Never Say Die!* and it was the worst piece of work that I've ever had anything to do with," he said. "I'm ashamed of that album. I think it's disgusting."

21

GOODBYE TO ROMANCE

SABBATH FIRES OZZY

APRIL 27, 1979

After the ignominious end of the *Never Say Die!* tour, the members of Black Sabbath rented a house in Bel Air to write their next album. The last time they had gone there, the end result had been the acclaimed *Vol. 4* album, so they may have chosen that location to capture lightning in a bottle again.

The problems that had plagued the making of their last album had not gone away. Tony Iommi wrote in his memoir that everyone in the band was too into drugs and alcohol to be productive, but the singer was "on a totally different level altogether." Osbourne was also flatly refusing to sing over the few ideas his bandmates would actually come up with, leaving the proceedings at an impasse.

Iommi wrote that the only choices were to fire Ozzy or break up the band. He chose the former, and he asked drummer Bill Ward, who was close with the singer, to do the honors. According to *I Am Ozzy*, the reasons Ward gave for the firing were that the singer was unreliable and too perpetually drunk and/or stoned. However, it's worth mentioning that in the memoir, Osbourne said that his consumption of substances was at around the same level as everyone else's.

When he was ousted from the band, Osbourne believed that his career was now functionally over, and there wasn't a future to look forward to. He had been paid out for his share, and it wasn't a lot of money—just enough for him to rot away.

"I'd got £96,000 for my share of the name, so I'd just locked myself away and spent three months doing coke and booze," he told *Classic Rock* in 2002. "My thinking was, 'This is my last party because after this I'm going back to Birmingham and the dole.'"

It's hard not to feel sorry for Osbourne post-firing. The group had made two albums that they weren't jazzed about, and on the *Never Say Die!* tour, they

were blown offstage nightly by a crew of young, energetic upstarts called Van Halen. Sabbath was old, Van Halen was young, and that's life. One must wonder if those factors, more than the drugs and alcohol, hadn't been the impetus for the "something has to change" sentiment that resulted in his firing.

The band members have frequently contradicted one another over the years. Between their different perceptions— all of which were colored by substance abuse—it's unlikely that there will ever be a single definitive version of the reasons

for the firing. However, in 1996's *The Story of Black Sabbath: Wheels of Confusion*, the man who had to break the bad news to Osbourne placed the majority of the blame on alcohol.

"Alcohol was definitely one of the most damaging things to Black Sabbath," he said. "We were destined to destroy each other. The band were toxic, very toxic."

Ozzy with Black Sabbath on the 1978 *Never Say Die!* tour, which probably should have been called the *Die!* tour.

PART 3

FLYING HIGH AGAIN, 1979—1989

Ozzy in 1982, thrusting aloft the dude who gave him a whole new career after Sabbath.

22

"GET YOUR SH*T TOGETHER"

SHARON ARDEN MEETS HER FUTURE HUSBAND

DATE UNKNOWN, 1979

Ozzy with manager Sharon Arden in 1982, a few months before he put a ring on it and made her Mrs. Osbourne.

When Ozzy Osbourne was excused from further vocal duties in Black Sabbath, the band were managed by Don Arden, who had picked up where the fired Patrick Meehan had left off. Arden's reputation for doing things that may or may not have been legal preceded him. His 2007 obituary in the *Guardian* referred to him as "the Al Capone of pop," after all.

His daughter, Sharon Arden, had worked for him since her teenage years, and according to her, the nickname was appropriate. In a 2007 interview with the television show *Shrink Rap*, she said that violence was a daily fixture in her family life, to such an extent that it didn't even seem unusual to her.

"I was surrounded by violent people, violent talk, violent behavior, so there was nothing unusual seeing my dad threatening someone or brandishing a firearm," she said. "It seemed normal. I thought everybody was like this. It was part of our lives."

Sharon has never been said to be tied to organized crime figures, so in that sense, she broke away from her father's way of doing things. However, her rage is the stuff of legend, and you don't have to look far to see the inspiration for it.

"My father really had a temper," she told *Shrink Rap*. "He had a voice which would echo through the entire house. A couple of times, he would whack me, and he used to yank my hair. I wouldn't say I was abused and beaten; in those days, it was a normal thing."

After Ozzy's firing, Don Arden signed him to Jet Records, who put him up at Le Parc Hotel in West Hollywood. With the last of his Black Sabbath money, Osbourne financed a months-long kamikaze mission of drugs, alcohol, and pizza that was only interrupted when fellow Jet Records artist Mark Nauseef told him that Don's daughter, Sharon, was coming to collect an envelope. Could the singer take time out from his busy schedule to give it to her?

Ozzy accepted the challenge and said in his memoir that he opened the envelope, found $500 inside, and promptly blew it all on cocaine. Soon after, she came by to pick up the cash, quickly figured out what had happened, and gave him what he referred to as a "monumental bollocking." He figured he would never see her again, but in fact, she came back the next day to find him "lying in a puddle of my own piss, smoking a joint."

"If you ever want to get your shit together, we want to manage you," she said.

The "we" meant Sharon and her father, but she quickly began to assert more

control over Ozzy's career, much to Dad's chagrin. That led to a rift between father and daughter, and the relationship was never repaired. But for Ozzy and Sharon, it was day one.

In 1985, an era long before Beavis and Butthead did America, Ozzy and Sharon did Brazil.

23

"YOU CAN'T KILL ROCK AND ROLL"

OZZY MEETS RANDY RHOADS

NOVEMBER 27, 1979

During the *Blizzard of Ozz* sessions, Ozzy witnessed Randy Rhoads perform one superhuman guitar feat after another.

PART 4: RETIREMENT SUCKS, 1990-1998

Ozzy releases the live album *Just Say Ozzy*.

1990
MARCH 17

40

Ozzy releases *No More Tears* as the musical landscape changes.

1991
SEPTEMBER 17

41

Ozzy announces that his 1992 tour will be his last.

1992
NOVEMBER 15

42

Ozzy releases *Live & Loud*, allegedly his final live album.

1993
JUNE 28

43

Retirement goes so well for Ozzy that he goes back on tour two years later.

1995
JUNE 9

44

Ozzy releases *Ozzmosis* in the middle of the grunge era.

1995
OCTOBER 23

45

The first Ozzfest takes place.

1996
OCTOBER 25

46

The original Sabbath lineup reunites for the first time since 1985's Live Aid.

1997
DECEMBER 4

47

Black Sabbath releases the *Reunion* live album.

1998
OCTOBER 20

48

PART 5: "SHAAAARON!!!!", 2001-2007

Ozzy releases *Down to Earth*, his first new album of the century.

2001
OCTOBER 16

49

As if to confirm that he's not retired, Ozzy releases *Live at Budokan*.

2002
FEBRUARY 15

50

The Osbournes premieres on MTV, giving Ozzy and family a whole new fan base.

2002
MARCH 5

51

Ozzy's first two LPs are reissued with the original rhythm tracks replaced.

2002
APRIL 2

52

Ozzy meets the President of the United States.

2002
MAY 4

53

Sharon Osbourne is diagnosed with cancer. She beats it.

2002
JULY 3

54

Ozzy gets prescribed a mountain of painkillers, which rarely has a happy ending.

2003
DECEMBER 7

55

Ozzy has an accident on his quad bike that will affect his health for years to come.

2003
DECEMBER 8

56

Ozzy releases the *Prince of Darkness* box set, half of which is great.

2005
MARCH 22

57

Ozzy becomes a spokesman for I Can't Believe It's Not Butter!

2006
FEBRUARY 20

58

Black Sabbath is inducted into the Rock and Roll Hall of Fame.

2006
MARCH 13

59

Ozzy releases *Black Rain*, his first record made while sober.

2007
MAY 22

60

PART 6: WRITIN', REUNIONS, AND RETIREMENTS, 2010-2019

Ozzy's memoir, *I Am Ozzy*, is released to an unsuspecting public.

2010
JANUARY 25

61

Ozzy releases *Scream*; fans rejoice that it's not called *Soul Sucka*.

2010
JUNE 11

62

Scientists examine Ozzy to glean insights as to why he's still alive.

2010
JUNE 15

63

Ozzy and Sharon's home is featured in *Architectural Digest*.

2011
JUNE 1

64

Sabbath's original lineup chooses the heaviest day in history to announce their reformation.

2011
NOVEMBER 11

65

Black Sabbath releases *13*, their first album with Ozzy in thirty-five years.

2013
JUNE 10

66

Ozzy gets a tram named after him in Birmingham.

2016
MAY 27

67

The Osbournes return to TV with *Ozzy & Jack's World Detour*.

2016
JULY 24

68

RIP Black Sabbath (1968–2017). They told you they were sick.

2017
MARCH 7

69

Ozzy embarks on *No More Tours II*, the longest farewell tour in history.

2018
APRIL 27

70

Ozzy releases "Take What You Want" with Post Malone and hits the charts.

2019
OCTOBER 15

71

PART 7: LIVIN' LA VIDA LOCKDOWN, 2020-2022

Ozzy is diagnosed with Parkinson's disease, which sucks no matter how you slice it.

2020
JANUARY 21

72

Defying the haters, Ozzy releases *Ordinary Man*, his first solo album in a decade.

2020
FEBRUARY 21

73

Ozzy and Jack celebrate being sober for a long stretch of years.

2021
FEBRUARY 5

74

Ozzy and Sharon get the dreaded COVID-19 virus, but it does not hasten their demise.

2022
MAY 5

75

Ozzy releases *Patient Number 9*, defying the critics, death, and logic.

2022
SEPTEMBER 9

75.666

PART 1: OZZY ZIG SEEKS GIG, 1948–1969

A bat-biting dove-destroyer is born.

1948
DECEMBER 3

01

Ozzy meets the Beatles. Sort of.

1963
AUGUST 23

02

Ozzy goes to jail. He would be back.

1966

03

Ozzy and three fellow Brummies start maiming innocent eardrums.

1968
DECEMBER 11

04

Ozzy et. al. pick a name that sticks—Black Sabbath.

1969
AUGUST 9

05

PART 2: BEHIND THE WALL OF SLEEP, 1970–1979

Black Sabbath's self-titled debut is released.

1970
FEBRUARY 13

06

The Sabs get invited to Stonehenge a decade before Spinal Tap.

1970

07

Black Sabbath releases their sophomore outing, *Paranoid.* The world never recovers.

1970
SEPTEMBER 18

08

Ozzy meets his first wife. By his own admission, he made a hash of the marriage.

1971

09

Black Sabbath releases *Master of Reality,* their heaviest album yet.

1971
JULY 21

10

Ozzy's first child is born. For a while there, it was nice.

1972
JANUARY 20

11

The boys snort their way through the recording of their next album.

1972
MAY

12

The cocaine-fueled *Vol. 4* album is released.

1972
SEPTEMBER 25

13

Ozzy and friends visit a local hospital to treat their diseased genitals.

1972

14

A local vicar unwittingly eats a cake Ozzy made with hash. Oops.

1973

15

The band releases *Sabbath Bloody Sabbath.*

1973
DECEMBER 1

16

The band releases *Sabotage* as the rot sets in.

1975
JULY 28

17

A drunken Ozzy goes apeshit with a gun on some innocent chickens.

1976

18

Black Sabbath releases *Technical Ecstasy,* and the wheels start coming off the bus.

1976
SEPTEMBER 25

19

Black Sabbath releases their last album with Ozzy for many moons, *Never Say Die!*

1978
SEPTEMBER 28

20

Ozzy gets fired from Black Sabbath. Everything sucks. Boo, hiss.

1979
APRIL 27

21

PART 3: FLYING HIGH AGAIN, 1979–1989

At his lowest point, Ozzy meets his future wife.

1979

22

A solo Ozzy enlists wunderkind guitarist Randy Rhoads.

1979
NOVEMBER 27

23

Ozzy releases his solo debut, *Blizzard Of Ozz.* If you don't like it, you're stupid.

1980
SEPTEMBER 15

24

Ozzy bites the head off at least two doves during a business meeting.

1981
MARCH 27

25

Ozzy and Sharon visit the Fatherland, where goose-stepping jokes are not appreciated.

1981

26

Ozzy's second solo album, *Diary of a Madman,* is released.

1981
NOVEMBER 7

27

Ozzy bites the head off a dead bat. He never lives it down.

1982
JANUARY 20

28

Ozzy voids his bladder on sacred terrain—the Alamo.

1982
FEBRUARY 19

29

Randy Rhoads dies in a plane crash along with a member of the band's crew.

1982
MARCH 19

30

Ozzy releases the *Speak of the Devil* live album. Some of it is live, anyway.

1982
NOVEMBER 27

31

Ozzy releases *Bark at the Moon,* his first album with guitarist Jake E. Lee.

1983
NOVEMBER 15

32

Ozzy schools Mötley Crüe in proper poolside behavior and interior design for hotels.

1984
MAY 19

33

Ozzy is sued over alleged backward masking, leading to a fan's suicide.

1984
OCTOBER 26

34

Ozzy releases *The Ultimate Sin,* album number two with Jake E. Lee.

1986
FEBRUARY 22

35

Ozzy releases the live album *Tribute* in Randy Rhoads' honor.

1987
MARCH 19

36

Ozzy is mistakenly diagnosed with HIV. What a boner!

1987

37

Ozzy releases *No Rest for the Wicked,* with new guitarist Zakk Wylde.

1988
SEPTEMBER 28

38

While extremely shitfaced, Ozzy nearly murders Sharon.

1989
SEPTEMBER 3

39

Ozzy wrote in his memoir that after he was fired from Black Sabbath, Don Arden had lots of ideas about what career path he should take next. He hated all of them, and with good reason. One idea was for Ozzy to front a band called "Son of Sabbath," and another was for the singer and his former band to tour together and have one go on after the other. On the other hand, Sharon was interested in treating the singer like a legitimate artist in his own right. She suggested that he start his own band to back him as a solo artist.

As far as the rhythm section was concerned, he filled those slots with former Rainbow bassist Bob Daisley and former Uriah Heep drummer Lee Kerslake. Both men were seasoned rock veterans who had already traveled the world with their respective bands. But for the all-important guitar slot, Osbourne picked a young unknown named Randy Rhoads.

At that time, Rhoads was a member of Quiet Riot. Even though he was only twenty-two when he met Osbourne, he was already an accomplished guitarist, studying formally since childhood. More importantly, he sounded nothing like Tony Iommi at all. His clean, classically influenced playing was a completely different animal from Iommi's more blues-influenced style. It set Ozzy apart not just from Black Sabbath but from the entire classic rock sound of the 1970s. If Osbourne was looking to move on from what had come before, Rhoads was the perfect vehicle for it.

Dana Strum of Slaughter introduced the guitarist to Osbourne in Los Angeles. Before the audition, Rhoads started warming up. Osbourne stopped him seconds later to tell him he was hired.

"You should have heard him play, man," he said in his memoir. "I almost cried, he was so good."

Osbourne said that, unlike Tony Iommi, Rhoads would sit down with him and work on ideas. He would do things like find keys to work in that favored his vocal range. He also said the guitarist had a style that shared some finger-tapping DNA with what people like Eddie Van Halen were doing, but he was more versatile and more able to throw in a dash of blues or a dash of classical. The young guitarist was simply a one-off, as the Brits say.

"I remember when Randy did the solo for 'I Don't Know,' my head spun around on my shoulders," he told *Rolling Stone* in 2021. "And the solo at the end of 'Mr. Crowley' was awesome; it's in the same category as Pink Floyd's 'Comfortably Numb.' When you hear something like that, you know you've discovered somebody who is a somewhat more-than-normal guy."

Rhoads's life was cut short in a 1982 plane crash when he was only twenty-five. If he were alive today, he would be in his sixties, and it's anyone's guess what he would have accomplished had he lived. Many people close to Osbourne have said that he never really recovered from Rhoads's death, and considering the guitarist's role in giving Osbourne an Act Two, that makes sense.

"He was a great player," Osbourne said in 2021. "I owe my career to him."

24

OZZY OSBOURNE— *BLIZZARD OF OZZ*

OZZY'S SOLO DEBUT IS A STRAIGHT BANGER

SEPTEMBER 15, 1980

Ozzy Osbourne's 1980 debut solo album *Blizzard of Ozz* had a job to do—it had to prove that there was life after Black Sabbath for the singer. Today, it seems absurd that it was even a question, but at the time, the future of "Black Sabbath's old singer" was very much in doubt.

It takes about ten seconds of the opening track, "I Don't Know," to understand that there was never anything to worry about on that score. Rather than trying to one-up his old band and make music that competed with theirs, Ozzy wisely chose players to back him who sounded utterly different, and that's apparent pretty much the minute the record starts playing.

It's not exactly a secret, but to the extent that this album had a secret weapon, it was Randy Rhoads. Bassist Bob Daisley and drummer Lee Kerslake form a rock-solid rhythm section with less swing and a more hard rock edge than Butler-Ward, which serves the songs well, but the star here is Randy Rhoads. His guitar playing is so inventive and refreshing that it has the effect of someone throwing open the curtains in a darkened room at midday. That feeling lasts for the record's entire thirty-nine-minute running time.

There are no bad songs anywhere on the album, and more than half of it is absolutely indispensable. Apart from

Ozzy and Randy Rhoads lay waste to New York City's Palladium in 1981.

fear of nuclear war that many people could identify with at the time. It's distinguished by its main riff, which is easily as iconic as that of "Iron Man" or "Smoke on the Water" but never appeared on any guitar store signs forbidding potential customers from playing it, most likely because it's beyond the reach of the aspiring player with only a lesson or two under their belt.

"Crazy Train" is now over forty years old, and Osbourne still performs it at every concert. In 2019, he told *Blabbermouth* that his granddaughter Pearl sang it at her school in a variety show about the 1980s. As much as the Moral Majority and Tipper Gore might have wanted to wipe the music of Ozzy Osbourne and everyone like him off the airwaves, there's no defeating a great song, and this one has been passed down from generation to generation. There's no reason to believe the song, or the album it first appeared on, will fade out of human memory any time soon.

"I Don't Know," there's "Goodbye to Romance," a ballad inspired by Osbourne's departure from his previous band. "Suicide Solution" is a stomper that was inspired by the death of AC/DC's Bon Scott, and the album closer "Steal Away (The Night)" has an ascending chromatic chord sequence during the choruses that will inspire involuntary headbanging in the listener.

The proceedings are only slightly reminiscent of Osbourne's old band during "Mr. Crowley," whose opening keyboard sequence—courtesy of Don Airey—starts the song off ominously before the whole band kicks in. Ozzy asks Mr. Crowley "what went on in your head" in the plaintive wail that only he can produce. Oh, and did we fail to mention that Randy Rhoads's guitar solo on this song is some of the most adept and musical shredding you're ever going to hear?

If *Blizzard of Ozz* is known for any one song, it's "Crazy Train," a meditation on the

Ozzy poses with the second incarnation of his backing band (from left, bassist Rudy Sarzo, guitarist Randy Rhoads, Ozzy, and drummer Tommy Aldridge).

25

WHEN DOVES DIE

OZZY MAKES AN UNFORGETTABLE IMPRESSION ON THE SUITS AT CBS

MARCH 27, 1981

It was March 27, 1981, and Ozzy Osbourne and his manager Sharon Arden had come to Los Angeles to meet with the top brass at CBS Records. His solo debut, *Blizzard of Ozz*, had come out in England the previous year, and it was about to get its U.S. release courtesy of CBS. Sharon felt that his relationship with the U.S. label executives would probably get off to a smoother start if he met everyone in person.

"The deal was he was to go in, because it was his first introduction to the record company," Sharon said on the *Wild Ride! with Steve-O* podcast in 2020. "The deal was done. It was okay, this is Ozzy. You've just signed him. It was like a meet and greet, a quick meet and greet. It was just like 'hi,' and that was it."

She said that at this point, it was important that the executives put a face to his name because he was still fighting the perception that he was Black Sabbath's old, washed-up, fired singer. He needed to make a positive impression on his own. Unfortunately, as they played the *Blizzard of Ozz* record for the suits, it was clear that they weren't really paying much attention. Luckily, she had given the singer two live doves, one for each jacket pocket. She had the idea to release them into the room to the childlike delight of the executives, who would then give him more attention as a result.

"So Ozzy goes in, he's already drunk, and it's morning," Sharon recalled. "He sits on this girl's lap who he has no idea who she is . . . he takes the dove out, and he just rips the head off and spits it on the girl's lap. . . . He then gets the other one and lets the other one free in the room, so it's flying and shitting in the room."

While the incident is one of Ozzy's most legendary, it was hard in the moment to see that he had just stepped into the history books. According to Sharon,

Ozzy during the *Diary of a Madman* photo shoot, surrounded by props that did not help him shed his image as He-Who-Cannot-Be-Named.

after the incident, she and her future husband were told how CBS Records felt about it in no uncertain terms.

"I got a call from legal," she recalled. "They said, 'If you ever do this again, we won't release the album, and we'll literally destroy you.'"

Osbourne remembered the incident a little differently, telling author Mick Wall in *Black Sabbath: Symptom of the Universe* that he had actually decapitated two

doves that fateful morning and had spit out the head of the second one onto the conference room table. Whatever really happened and however many doves it happened to, the story became instantly legendary, and Sharon said in Wall's book that *Blizzard of Ozz* began flying off of record store shelves almost immediately.

Fun Fact: In 2022, bassist Rudy Sarzo, who joined Osbourne's band on the same 1981 day as the Day of the Dove, told *Yahoo!* that after the meeting at

CBS, Ozzy told him what had happened. "And as we were talking, I see that his jacket is flapping," Sarzo said. "I go, 'What's that?' And he puts his hand in his pocket, pulls out another bird, looks at it, and he just goes and bites the head off again—right in front of me!"

26

ICH LIEBE DICH, SHARON! SEI MEINE FRAU!

OZZY AND SHARON INVADE GERMANY

DATE UNKNOWN, 1981

A few days before the *Blizzard of Ozz* tour was set to begin, Ozzy Osbourne finally achieved his dream of engaging with Sharon Arden in the physical act of love. Or, as he put it so eloquently in his memoir, "I got Sharon in the sack for the first time." He said that she had gone to take a bath, he jumped in the tub with her, and they were off to the races. Sadly, he does not detail the number of candles lit, the type of smooth jazz played in the background, or the number of rose petals that he used to wipe away her tears of ecstasy. But we're all adults here, and we can fill in the blanks ourselves.

Osbourne said that what was most striking to him even before the relationship became romantic was how similar he and Sharon were. In other words, anywhere they went, they were always the two drunkest and loudest people there, which does not sound like a great deal for anyone else who happened to be within shrieking distance.

One such event took place in Germany. They were attending a dinner with the head of CBS Europe on the occasion of the German release of *Blizzard of Ozz*. Osbourne described the label head as "a big, bearded, cigar-chomping bloke, and very straight," and himself as utterly shitfaced.

In the middle of the dinner, the singer climbed on top of the table and started stripping. He describes it as a "striptease" in the memoir, but it's less likely that he was engaged in the erotic art of burlesque and more likely that he was a drunk standing on a table while everyone was just trying to eat their *Wienerschnitzel*. He recalled that once he was free of his garments, he made a number one in the label chief's wine carafe, then kissed him on the lips. As one does.

Amazingly, his recollection of what he did was not 100 percent accurate. As he and Sharon left Germany, she commented that thanks to Ozzy's stunt, they could cross that country off the list of places where he could get airplay, since they

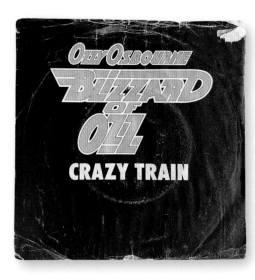

could now count on no label support whatsoever. Ozzy commented that it had been "worth it for the striptease," and Sharon informed him that no such event had occurred.

"That wasn't a striptease you were doing, Ozzy," she said. "It was a fucking Nazi goosestep. Up and down the table. That poor German bloke looked mortified. Then you put your balls in his fucking wine."

Osbourne was shocked and said he thought he had only pissed in the man's wine, as if that's better somehow. Sharon informed him that he had, in fact, urinated in the guy's wine, but only *after* dipping his testicles into it. So no matter what Ozzy Osbourne does in life and no matter what happens to him, no one can ever take that achievement away from him.

Ozzy and Sharon at the Heavy Metal Holocaust concert in 1981. What's that in the cup, wheatgrass juice?

DIARY OF A MADMAN

OZZY'S SECOND SOLO ALBUM THRILLS AND DELIGHTS

NOVEMBER 7, 1981

In 1981, Ozzy and bassist Rudy Sarzo inform the crowd at New York City's Palladium that try as one might, you can't kill rock and roll.

Released in November 1981, Ozzy Osbourne's follow-up to his solo debut, *Diary of a Madman*, is almost on par with the album that preceded it. With the debut, Osbourne had something to prove, and between that and his game-changing relationship with guitarist Randy Rhoads, the record crackled with palpable excitement. That same "first time jumping out of an airplane" feeling is not quite there, but the "second time jumping out of an airplane" feeling is still pretty exhilarating.

Musically, not much changed between the first album and the second. Despite the album credits, the personnel is the same (more on that later). As with *Diary of a Madman*, the guitar playing does most of the heavy lifting while the rhythm section keeps it simple and sturdy. It

opens with "Over the Mountain," whose upbeat arrangement recalls *Piece of Mind*–era Iron Maiden, but for Ozzy's unmistakable voice.

"Flying High Again" flirts with pop during the choruses, and the seven-minute "You Can't Kill Rock and Roll" is a lesson in how to write a multipart epic track with different textures and dynamics without falling into the aimlessness that had plagued Ozzy's last couple of Sabbath albums. The only thing remotely approaching "dud" status is the side one closer, "Believer," although it's somewhat redeemed by its sophisticated middle section.

After side two opens with "Little Dolls," the album ends in grand style with three consecutive masterpieces. "Tonight" finds Ozzy in semi-ballad territory, singing melodies that simply would never have emerged during his time in Sabbath. You could almost use the words "tender" or "heartfelt" if it wasn't the same guy that just months earlier had decapitated as many as three innocent birds.

"S.A.T.O." is an energetic rocker based around a shuffle beat, the kind drummer Lee Kerslake had been playing ad nauseam with Uriah Heep. Rumor has it that the title stands for "Sharon Arden Thelma Osbourne," the two women in Ozzy's life at the time, although it could also stand for "Scheduled Airlines Ticket Office" or "Student Athletic Trainers Organization."

The album wraps up with the profoundly addictive title track, a dark meditation on sinking into insanity. It's the best song on the album, and it's the kind of song you can put on endless repeat and listen to forever, because you will never, ever get sick of it. Also, the guitar riff at about the 4:15 mark is brilliant, and the fact that it only goes around a couple of times will have you returning to those grooves over and over again until you die. The song ends with a choral section that sounds a hell of a lot like "Supertzar," and it's tempting to wonder if that wasn't a conscious choice intended by Ozzy to stick it to his former band.

If *Diary of a Madman* isn't quite the A+ that *Blizzard of Ozz* was, it's damn close, and it manages to take what was good about the previous album and expand on it without sounding like a rehash. It also reinforced that Ozzy was now officially his own entity and was no longer a "formerly of." Sadly, Randy Rhoads would lose his life just a few months after the album's release, so we'll never know what the third album with his contributions would have sounded like.

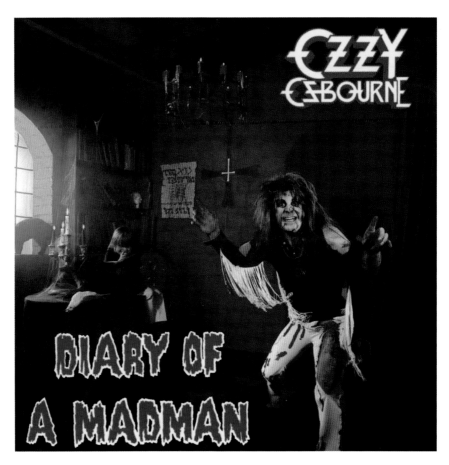

28

OZZY AT THE BAT

**THE BAT STORY.
NEED WE SAY MORE?**

JANUARY 20, 1982

January 20, 1982, was, much like December 7, 1941, a day that will live in infamy. It was the day Ozzy Osbourne bit the head off a bat during a concert date in Des Moines, and for the last forty-plus years, that's been the thing that everyone knows about him, even people who don't listen to his music. His musical career may have moved on from that moment, but the public's memory never did, and more than four decades later, we're still talking about it.

According to the *Des Moines Register*, the incident occurred when a kid named Mark Neal came to Osbourne's concert at the Veterans Memorial Auditorium with a dead bat in tow, courtesy of his little brother. The younger lad had somehow acquired the winged rodent and tried to make it a pet, and as often happens with minors and intended pets, the creature sadly perished. The *Register* is a little unclear about the bat's cause of death, so let's just say it died and move on.

Long story short, Ozzy takes the stage, Mark throws the dead bat up there, and

thinking it's fake, Ozzy picks it up and bites its head off. And from there, a legend was born.

Osbourne had to be rushed to a hospital and treated for rabies. The nurse supervisor at the hospital, Pam Culver, said that even though she didn't treat Osbourne directly that night, she dealt with the aftermath long after his tour bus left for the next town.

"For a week, that was probably 50% of my job—fielding calls from England and Canada and all over the United States," she told the *Register*. "People wanted to know how much did it cost to do that, and did it hurt, and how many shots did he have to have, what part of his body did we have to attack."

After the incident, Veterans Memorial Auditorium changed its policies, prohibiting performers "from using, presenting or in any way making live animals a part of a program at Vets without the consent of management." It was a concertgoer that threw the bat

onstage, but perhaps the venue so feared Osbourne making bat-decapitation a permanent part of his act that they just wanted to nip it in the bud right then and there.

Osbourne has had a laudable attitude toward the entire affair and has allowed bat-centric merchandise bearing his image and likeness to fill store shelves. An Ozzy action figure was manufactured in 1999 that came with little headless bats, and in 2019, the singer announced that the thirty-seventh anniversary of the incident was being celebrated with an Ozzy-branded plush bat toy with a detachable head.

If Ozzy had any worries that the bat incident would overshadow his musical accomplishments, his approval of merchandise glorifying it would seem to indicate otherwise. Besides, he told *Esquire* in 2005 that ship had already sailed long ago.

"I know what's going to be on my tombstone, and there's no getting around it," he said. "'Here lies Ozzy Osbourne, the ex-Black Sabbath singer who bit the head off a bat.'"

Ozzy in 1984, two years after accepting the fact that the bat thing would hound him for the rest of his life.

29

TEXAS UNDER SIX FLAGS

THE STARS AT NIGHT ARE BIG AND BRIGHT

Greetings from SAN ANTONIO TEXAS

OZZY PAYS A VISIT TO THE ALAMO

FEBRUARY 19, 1982

The Alamo Mission, which most people just call the Alamo, is located in the Texas city of San Antonio. In 1836, it was the site of the Battle of the Alamo, where Davy Crockett lost his life. It's a site of great historical interest and pride for the people of the Lone Star state, although to this day, it has no basement, making stolen bicycle storage impossible.

On February 19, 1982, Ozzy Osbourne put on one of Sharon's dresses and urinated on the Alamo Cenotaph, a monument to the Battle of the Alamo that's adjacent to the Alamo itself and is not actually connected to the building. However, even decades before the internet, the incident immediately turned into "Ozzy Osbourne pissed on the Alamo."

Osbourne was banned from performing in San Antonio, and the incident could

have become just another in a long line of stories about stunts that he pulled while drunk. However, a decade later, both singer and city decided that enough tears had been shed, and it was time for healing.

In 1992, Osbourne issued a public apology to the city and sweetened the deal with a $10,000 donation to the Daughters of the Republic of Texas. This organization maintains the Alamo grounds, including the monument he had used as his target while taking a tinkle. The city kindly and graciously accepted his apology (and, one assumes, his money) and gave him the go-ahead to perform two nights in the city that had once banned him.

"We all have done things in our lives that we regret," he said in a public statement. "I am deeply honored that

Sharon springs Ozzy from the Bexar County Adult Detention Center on February 19, 1982, after he was arrested for urinating on the Alamo Cenotaph.

the people of San Antonio have found it in their hearts to have me back. I hope that this donation will show that I have grown up."

Not surprisingly, some saw the original episode not as a stain on Osbourne's immaculate record but rather as something worth celebrating. The incident, which *Loudwire* described as "Osbourne's San Antonio wee-wee infraction," became an instant legend in Ozzy lore, and it inspired local artists Jim Mendiola and Ruben Ortiz-Torres to create an installation called "Fountain/ Ozzy Visits The Alamo."

The installation consisted of a wax replica of Osbourne. Thanks to the miracle of motion-detection technology, passersby would trigger the life-size wax figure, and it would "urinate" on a wall, recreating this vital moment in music history several times a day.

In 2015, Osbourne and his son Jack returned to San Antonio, where he was greeted by one hundred fans who saw him not as a vandal who had been careless with his renal waste but as a conquering hero. Even local councilman Roberto Treviño, whose district included San Antonio, showed up and graciously welcomed the former pee-pee terrorist back to the state that had once banned him.

"Certainly, as a city, we feel very, very good about his efforts to come to our great city and apologize for the actions of a not-so-sober person," the councilman said.

30

DEATH OF A DREAM

AN ACCIDENT KILLS RANDY RHOADS AND RACHEL YOUNGBLOOD

MARCH 19, 1982

Randy Rhoads plays one astounding lick after another at an Ozzy concert in 1981. He would be dead less than a year later.

Randy Rhoads played his final concert in Knoxville, Tennessee, on March 18, 1982. The next scheduled date on the *Diary of a Madman* tour was in Orlando, and on the way, the tour bus stopped at a depot in Leesburg, Florida, to fix the air conditioning. According to Ozzy's memoir, the depot was part of a "dodgy housing estate" with an airstrip and small planes. Andrew Aycock, the tour bus driver, was also a pilot, and Osbourne said that Aycock had been powering the long overnight drives with cocaine.

Aycock decided to take members of the band and crew up in a small plane that he had taken from the site without permission. First, he took keyboard player Don Airey and tour manager Jake Duncan up in the plane. During the flight, Aycock flew close to the tour bus in an attempt to "buzz" it, also known as flying super close to it so it makes an apocalyptically loud sound that scares the shit out of everyone on board. After that, the plane landed, and Rhoads and makeup artist Rachel Youngblood went up next.

Aycock buzzed the tour bus twice. The third time, one of its wings clipped the bus and the plane crashed, killing everyone on board.

Don Airey was standing outside the bus and saw everything that had happened. In Rudy Sarzo's memoir, Airey said he was taking pictures of the airplane with a telephoto lens. Before the crash, he saw a struggle between Rhoads and Aycock in the cockpit.

There has been a lot of speculation since the accident about Aycock's motives in trying to buzz the tour bus, with some eyewitnesses hypothesizing that he was trying to kill his ex-wife, who was on the bus, by crashing the plane into it. Sarzo, however, has a version of events that sadly seems the most plausible—Aycock was all fucked up from cocaine and lack of sleep, and people died as a result.

After a break, Rhoads was replaced by Bernie Tormé, then Night Ranger's Brad Gillis, and the *Diary of a Madman* tour finished up in August 1982. One month earlier, on July 4, Ozzy and Sharon got married. But the successful completion of the tour and the exchange of wedding vows weren't enough to wipe away the memory of what had happened. In an interview with *Ballbuster Music*, Don Airey said that Osbourne never really put the tragedy behind him.

"The sad thing about what happened that day is that it broke the whole thing apart, and no one ever really recovered from it," Airey said. "Ozzy never did."

31

SPEAK OF THE DEVIL

OZZY TRIES TO SOLDIER ON WITH A LIVE ALBUM

NOVEMBER 27, 1982

1982's *Speak of the Devil* was the first live album from a solo Ozzy Osbourne. It's been out of print for years, but for a lot of fans, it's a pillar of his catalog.

The original intention was to record a live album with Randy Rhoads. It was to consist entirely of Black Sabbath songs, mainly so that there would be publishing royalties to go around.

Ozzy's band at the time consisted of Rhoads, bassist Rudy Sarzo, and drummer Tommy Aldridge. They did not like the idea of making an album of Sabbath covers and refused to participate, leading Osbourne to fly into a drunken rage and fire the entire band. Luckily, he was so intoxicated that he had no memory of the event, and the

band grudgingly agreed to go ahead with the recording.

It was not to be. Rhoads died, and guitarist Brad Gillis was eventually drafted. Gillis, who would go on to be a member of Night Ranger, had the necessary pyrotechnic chops to split the difference between Rhoads's state-of-the-art technique and Tony Iommi's violent bludgeoning.

The album was scheduled to be recorded on September 26th and 27th of 1982 at the Ritz in New York City, and the band had all of five days to rehearse. Rudy Sarzo said in his memoir that Osbourne never showed up to rehearse, and none of the band members were in the same room with him until soundcheck on day one of the recording. Sarzo said that Osbourne

couldn't remember the lyrics to these songs that he had sung worldwide for a decade, so the singer put them in an open notebook on a folding chair at the front of the stage, illuminated by a desk lamp.

Producer Max Norman told KNAC in 2007 that he had the band perform their set to an empty Ritz on the afternoon of one of the two shows so there would be more material to draw from for the record. Things like crowd noise could be added later. Speaking of "added later," it's widely rumored that 100 percent of Osbourne's singing on *Speak of the Devil* was recorded in the studio well after the concert performances, and listening to the record would seem to bear that out. The singing all sounds fine and lovely, but the between-song banter sounds

like the demon from *The Exorcist* after chain-smoking a carton of Marlboro reds.

The results on *Speak of the Devil* are decidedly mixed. The band simply doesn't gel, but with five days of rehearsals without their employer present, they eke out a decent performance. Also, Brad Gillis, if you're reading this, you're not contractually obligated to use that whammy bar every ten seconds.

Although Osbourne has been dismissive of the album, it was helpful for one thing—it came out a month before Black Sabbath's *Live Evil* and outsold it. While his first two solo albums announced him as a star in his own right, this was the one that proved it wasn't a fluke, and he was here to stay.

Ozzy manages to look even more like a crazy person than usual with his freshly shaven head at New York City's Ritz in 1982.

This 1982 photo of a well-shorn Ozzy makes it very easy to conceptualize the fact that he once worked in an abattoir.

32

BARK AT THE MOON

NEW GUITARIST JAKE E. LEE JOINS THE FOLD

NOVEMBER 15, 1983

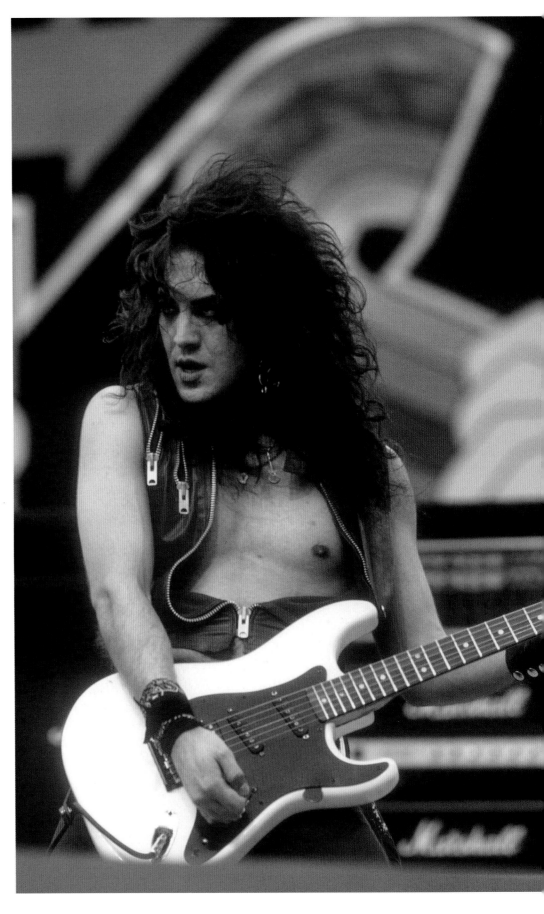

Somewhere in 1984, guitarist Jake E. Lee capably acquits himself of the thankless task of replacing Randy Rhoads.

When the *Bark at the Moon* LP was released in 1983, Ozzy Osbourne found himself in a situation similar to the one he was in after Sabbath. In 1979, he needed to prove that he had a future after his old band. Now, he had to prove something different. He needed to show that he could continue without Randy Rhoads and do so in the immediate aftermath of the very traumatic accident.

He had his work cut out for him. Osbourne and Rhoads had been perfect foils for one another, and the singer has said on many occasions that their partnership had been responsible for his career renaissance. So what's the verdict on his first post-Rhoads studio album, with Jake E. Lee as his new guitar player?

The results are mixed. The songwriting is credited to Osbourne alone, despite Lee telling *Trunk Nation* in 2014 that most of it was done by him, with an assist from bassist Bob Daisley. He said that Sharon Osbourne had given him an ultimatum—sign a contract denying any involvement in the songwriting and saying Ozzy wrote everything instead. He said they would just get another guitar player to record over his parts if he chose not to. As a young musician with no legal representation, he said he had little choice but to sign and hope for things to improve in the future.

As for the music itself, *Bark at the Moon* is much more pop than its predecessors, and the mix is weird as hell—it was remixed in 2002, so someone must have agreed. Guitar solos and keyboards are pushed way to the front, while Tommy Aldridge, one of the greatest rock drummers in the world, is completely buried. This is especially true on the song "So Tired," a ballad released in the UK as a single and which lays the violins on so thick it verges on parody. "You're No Different," a decent-enough ballad that follows the title track, suffers the same fate, with even Ozzy's voice getting

somewhat obscured by the mix. There are some good moments throughout, but they really suffer under the weight of the production.

The title track, which leads off the album, is the only thing that survives the mix and production in any sense. It's the best song on the record, and the closest thing to a peer that it has on the album is the closer, "Waiting for Darkness," which is similarly submerged in a morass of keyboards and sound effects. It gives the overall impression of someone who has overcooked dinner dumping sugar all over it, hoping that no one will notice.

Bark at the Moon has its moments but is a pretty frustrating listen overall. One kind of wishes there had been a little more of a "less is more" approach to the production, but then you realize this was 1983, and nobody who wanted to sell records in Ozzy quantities was going to do that. In that regard, the album did well, selling over three million copies in the U.S. But listening to it is significantly

less rewarding than listening to the two albums that preceded it, and there are just too many mediocre songs, like "Rock n' Roll Rebel," "Centre of Eternity," and the ballad, "So Tired."

After the album was done, Don Airey tendered his resignation. The keyboard player, who had seen the plane crash that had killed Randy Rhoads up close, told *Ballbuster Music* in 2004 that he left because Ozzy was at that point consuming so much drugs and alcohol that he just couldn't be around it anymore.

"I left the band because I said to Sharon, 'Ozzy's killing himself, and I don't want to be around another death in the band,'" he explained.

Why is Ozzy smiling? Because he found the perfect book about "Magick" to prop up that wobbly desk in the living room.

33

"HE'S PAINTING WITH IT"

OZZY SHOWS MÖTLEY CRÜE HOW IT'S DONE

MAY 19, 1984

To this day, Ozzy Osbourne's propensity for wild partying remains the stuff of legend. This is due in no small part to the fact that he did a lot of that partying in the pre-internet days when there was no ability to verify or debunk a story with a thirty-second trip to Snopes. Any story about any celebrity could become instantly plausible in those days.

One of the most notorious stories about Osbourne's partying appeared in the Mötley Crüe memoir *The Dirt: Confessions of the World's Most Notorious Rock Band*. It was 1984, and the Crüe had been chosen to support Osbourne on the *Bark at the Moon* tour. This opportunity afforded Nikki Sixx, Mick Mars, Tommy Lee, and Vince Neil a front-row seat to the antics of the Prince of Darkness at his most debauched.

As the story goes, the members of Mötley Crüe were catching some rays by the outdoor pool at a Lakeland, Florida, hotel in the middle of the tour. Osbourne appeared before them, and according to the lore, he was in the throes of a severe medical condition that doctors the world over describe as "being completely shitfaced."

Accounts vary as to what led up to it, but according to both the book and the 2019 Netflix movie adaptation,

Osbourne spied a line of live and very active ants on the pavement, grabbed a straw, and snorted them.

But wait, there's more! In both the book and the movie, Osbourne immediately got up after snorting the ants, urinated on the ground, and started licking it up. He challenged Mötley Crüe bassist Nikki Sixx to do the same, and he politely obliged, but after completing the urinating

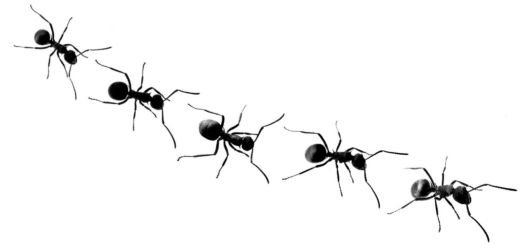

Ozzy with a bunch of snot-nosed young upstarts collectively known as Mötley Crüe in 1984, during which time he schooled them in the arts of advanced depravity.

BUFFALO MEMORIAL AUDITORIUM
BUFFALO, NEW YORK
JAN
28
1984
SATURDAY 7:30 P.M.
HARVEY and COPAY present
Another 97 Rock Concert Event
OZZY OSBOURNE
No Resale - No Refund
No Exchange

SEC/BX ROW SEAT
10 T LOWER BLUE 5
NO REFUND · NO EXCHANGE
Admission $12.50

portion of the afternoon, he was denied the opportunity to drink it all up greedily by Osbourne, who pushed him out of the way and started lapping up the golden nectar himself.

It's a crazy story, and in the annals of Osbourne's behavior, it's on-brand. However, in 2019, *Vanity Fair* asked a highly germane question about it that much of the news media had neglected—"Is it *true*?" According to both the book and the movie, it is. In fact, in the book, Sixx acknowledges Osbourne as someone who made them raise their game, depravity-wise.

"We thought we had elevated animal behavior to an art form," he wrote. "But then we met Ozzy."

Osbourne has never confirmed or denied that this event took place, and when asked about it, he gave an answer that's probably the most likely—"I have got absolutely no recollection of doing that." So it's less of a "he said, she said" situation and more of a "Crüe said, Ozzy doesn't remember" situation. Still, in a 2019 *Page Six* interview, Nikki Sixx said that it absolutely happened, and it had taught him and the rest of the band a valuable lesson.

"We were a wild young band, and he kind of took us under his wing," the bassist said. "We thought we could compete with that, but you can't with Ozzy. He won."

Fun Fact: Mötley Crüe drummer Tommy Lee recalled in the documentary *God Bless Ozzy Osbourne* that on that same tour, he had the privilege of being in Osbourne's hotel room when the singer dropped his pants and took a shit on the floor, then picked it up and started smearing it on the walls. "He's painting with it," the drummer recalled. "And I thought, 'This is some next-level shit. I'm not ready for this!' I'm cool with just taking a shit in the toilet."

Ozzy at an unidentified show sometime in the 1980s. If we're going by his hair, it's very possible that it's when Randy Rhoads was still sharing the stage with him.

34

THE "SUICIDE SOLUTION" LAWSUIT

OZZY SUED OVER BACKWARD MASKING

OCTOBER 26, 1984

For people who didn't live through the 1980s, it's hard to imagine how much power an artist like Ozzy Osbourne was believed to have over young minds. It was the era of Satanic Panic and backward masking, and many people legitimately believed that heavy metal music was behind every societal ill plaguing the teenagers of the world, from premarital intercourse to salty language and everything in between.

On October 26, 1984, a nineteen-year-old named John Daniel McCollum shot and killed himself at home. He was still wearing his headphones when he was found, and next to him on the turntable was *Speak of the Devil*, which does not actually include the song "Suicide Solution." Despite that, his parents sued Osbourne

and his label, CBS Records, claiming that the lyrics to "Suicide Solution" had driven the young man to take his own life.

Back on Earth, the song is actually a cautionary tale inspired by the alcohol-related death of AC/DC singer Bon Scott—alcohol is itself the "solution" in question, as a mixture of ethanol and water. But the grieving parents blamed their son's death on the lyrics to the song, and their attorney said that it contained the lyrics "get the gun and shoot," inspiring McCollum to do exactly that.

Surprisingly, one of the people who rushed to Osbourne's defense was his former manager and the father of his wife, Don Arden. According to Bob Daisley's website, Arden had said there was no way

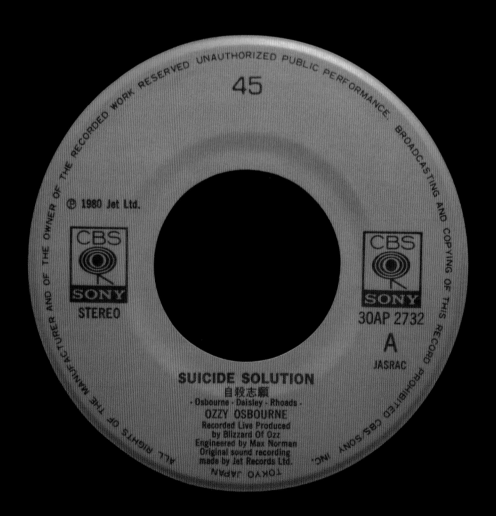

Ozzy at a 1986 press conference during the "Suicide Solution" trial, where he denied that his music caused a fan to take his own life.

Osbourne could have meant for the lyrics to inspire anyone to harm themselves. However, he said it in the most backhanded manner imaginable.

"To be perfectly honest, I would be doubtful as to whether Mr. Osbourne knew the meaning of the lyrics, if there was any meaning, because his command of the English language is minimal," Arden said.

The case was dismissed in 1988, partly because the lyrics enjoyed protection by the First Amendment and because it was impossible to draw a direct line between the song and McCollum's suicide. That same year, another family sued Osbourne and CBS Records over the same song after their son, Michael Jeffery Waller, died of a self-inflicted gunshot wound on May 3, 1986. That case was dismissed too.

At the time of McCollum's case, Osbourne went on record saying that the song was about the dangers of alcoholism and that while he was sympathetic to the young man, the lyrics had nonetheless been misinterpreted, if in fact they had even motivated him in the first place. He said he had sympathy for the parents but couldn't see that their conclusions had merit.

"The boy must have been pretty messed up before he ever heard an Ozzy record," he said in an interview at the time of the lawsuit. "I mean, I can't help that, you know? I feel very sad for the boy, and I felt terribly sad for the parents. As a parent myself, I'd be pretty devastated if something like that happened. And I have thought about this, if the boot was on the other foot, I couldn't blame the artist."

35

THE ULTIMATE SIN

OZZY'S SECOND LP WITH JAKE E. LEE IS A MIXED BAG

FEBRUARY 22, 1986

Ozzy in Chicago in 1986. For all you young ones, you used to have to dress this way in that decade or your earning potential would suffer.

1986's *The Ultimate Sin* was Ozzy Osbourne's biggest seller at the time of its release. It went platinum just three months after its release, and according to the Recording Industry Association of America, it went double platinum in 1994. All well and good, but Osbourne himself is actually not a fan. In 2019, he told *Rolling Stone* that he laid the fault for its shortcomings at the feet of its producer, Ron Nevison.

"[He] didn't really do a great production job," Osbourne said. "The songs weren't bad; they were just put down weird. Everything felt and sounded the fucking same. There was no imagination. If there was ever an album I'd like to remix and do better, it would be *The Ultimate Sin*."

A cursory listen to the album reveals that Osbourne may have been on to something. Leaving the music aside, the production is as 80s as it gets, with generous gated reverb on the drums, lots of high-gain lead guitar tones, and a snare drum that

has undergone the complete and utter removal of any kind of bite. This kind of production was par for the course in 1986, but it's aged horribly, and today it's hard to believe this was the bandwagon every artist wanted to jump on.

As for the music itself, the star of the show is guitarist Jake E. Lee. Whatever you can say about the production, the songwriting is mostly solid, and Lee's strengths as a riff master are on full display for the majority of the album's forty-one-minute running time—check out the opening riff on "Never," for example. He also acquits himself well of the type of shredding that was obligatory for any heavy metal guitarist at the time.

Not all of the music is great, of course. "Killer of Giants" is a very dated meditation on nuclear war, and "Lightning Strikes" is an abomination whose chorus about "rocking all night" causes embarrassment in the listener that's almost physically painful. In 2014, Lee told the *Trunk Nation*

satellite radio show that he had received no publishing or songwriting royalties for his contributions to *Bark at the Moon*, so he fought hard to get them on *The Ultimate Sin*. Having said that, "Lightning Strikes" is a song that he should have fought hard to have his name taken off.

On the whole, it's not bad. Every record has a couple of duds, and if anything sinks this one, it's the production more than the songs. If you've ever listened to Judas Priest's *Defenders of the Faith* album from 1984, you can hear a good album that's been hopelessly submerged by layer upon layer of over-production, and that's a good comparison point for *The Ultimate Sin*. The bad songs would have stopped it from being listed as one of Ozzy Osbourne's best albums, but the horrendous production job ensured that it would be counted among his worst, whether it deserved it or not.

Onstage with Jake E. Lee and in a more pensive moment backstage (opposite page) at Detroit's Joe Louis Arena, April 4, 1986.

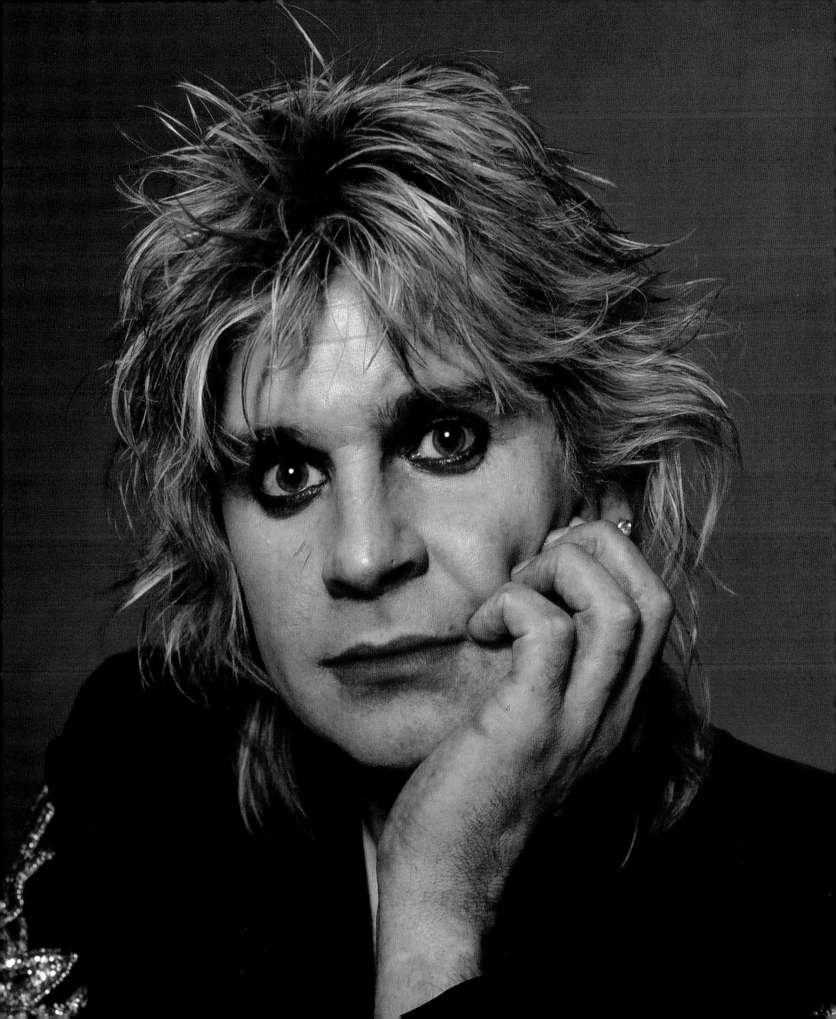

36

———————————————

TRIBUTE

———————————————

A LIVE ALBUM SHOWS RANDY RHOADS IN ALL HIS GLORY

———————————————

MARCH 19, 1987

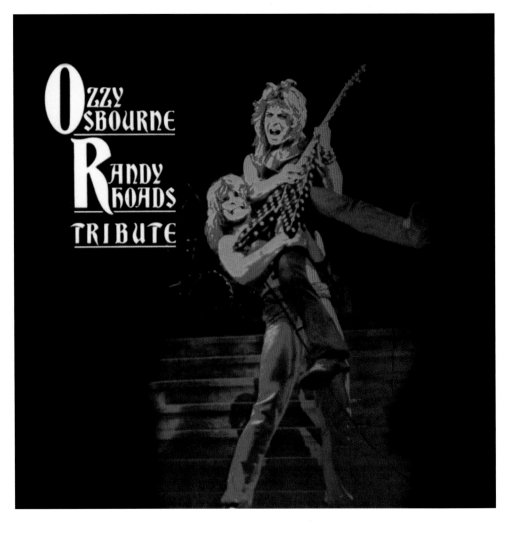

When Randy Rhoads passed away in 1982, it immediately stopped the plans that Ozzy and Co. had for the future. One of the plans was for a live album to be recorded in Toronto that same year, but the March 19, 1982, plane crash that killed Rhoads sidelined that.

Despite Ozzy's band moving on from the accident and the singer himself becoming a larger-than-life character, it always seemed remiss that there was no document of Rhoads's live playing. The absence of such a record always seemed like a glaring omission. This was rectified in 1987 with the release of *Tribute*, a live album from Rhoads's all-too-brief time as Ozzy's right-hand man. Most of it was recorded at a 1981 concert in Cleveland, and it primarily

focuses on the music he wrote with Ozzy, with a twelve-minute detour into Sabbath material in the middle of side three.

The playing is uniformly excellent from the jump, and it's a shocking reminder of how good this Randy Rhoads guy actually was. Bassist Rudy Sarzo and drummer Tommy Aldridge, who appear on the majority of the record, are certainly no slouches, and they play very well, but Rhoads seems to pull out one magic trick after another every five seconds, with every thirty-second-note run and bizarre extraterrestrial sound that he makes creating a distraction that's impossible to ignore. His playing also coaxes more energy out of Osbourne, who you can clearly tell is having the time of his life on stage with the young virtuoso.

The only lull on the entire album comes during the song "Steal Away (The Night)." The song itself is excellent and played at an almost hysterical pitch, and then it all goes away for a five-minute drum solo, which no one wants to hear. Unaccompanied drum solos are the worst things in the world, like sarin gas or ethnic cleansing, and they should appear nowhere in nature.

Luckily, it's followed by "Suicide Solution," which has an extended lead guitar break that somehow manages to elude the fate shared by so many others. In other words, you can listen to it without getting impatient. That makes Randy Rhoads one of a handful of guitar players, including Jimi Hendrix and Eddie Van Halen, who could play an unaccompanied solo without boring anyone.

The album ends with various takes of Rhoads performing the acoustic song "Dee." While there will never be enough of his music in the world, it rounds out the album in fine fashion. It all adds up to seventy-four minutes of inspiring and engaging music. While Rhoads's passing robbed the world of a stellar talent who clearly had decades of his best work ahead of him, *Tribute* is a fitting way of acknowledging his transformative effect on Ozzy Osbourne's career, as well as that of every aspiring guitarist on Earth.

Ozzy and Randy Rhoads wage war on the audience's eardrums at the Rosemount Horizon in January 1982.

DEATH TO FALSE POSITIVES

OZZY GETS AN AIDS SCARE

DATE UNKNOWN, 1987

In his 1980s heyday, Ozzy Osbourne enjoyed the company of groupies. As he said in his memoir, he wasn't unhappy in his marriage or anything like that. "I just wanted to think I was Robert Redford for an hour."

He was not deterred at first when AIDS burst onto the scene because he didn't think it applied to him. In those days, AIDS was believed by those outside of the medical community to be a "gay disease." It was thought that you could jab yourself with all the used syringes you wanted and face no consequences for it, provided you weren't gay when you did it.

That was the rationale under which Osbourne operated post-vasectomy. Sharon had told him she didn't want any more children after the three they had, and he went and got "the snip" per her request. This was a good deal for the singer, too, because now that he was shooting blanks, he could bed all the groupies he wanted without fear that they might turn up at his doorstep nine months later holding an eight-pound surprise that looked just like him.

After one such encounter at the Sunset Marquis Hotel in West Hollywood, Osbourne said he knew immediately that something was wrong. He had the front desk send up a doctor, who informed him that he should have an HIV test. Ozzy took the test, then had an agonizing week of waiting for the results. During that time, he admitted to Sharon what had happened, and she was not pleased, to say the least. Still, when the results came back, she went with him to the doctor to hear the news.

"Well, I'm afraid there's no easy way to tell you this," the doctor said. "But you're HIV positive."

In the 1980s, being told you had HIV was the same thing as being told you had AIDS—there was nothing they could do

for you, and you would likely go on to meet your great reward sooner than later. Ozzy and Sharon sat there absorbing the news when the doctor got a call. It was the lab, clarifying that the test was not "positive" but "borderline," meaning he would simply need to retake it. He did, and Sharon took one too, and they were both relieved when they came back negative. However, the reason for the false-positive test result was not much of an improvement on an HIV diagnosis. As the doctor told him, the singer's immune system had been so battered and abused by drugs and alcohol that it had stopped functioning.

"Your blood contains near-fatal quantities of alcohol and cocaine, Mr. Osbourne, not to mention a number of other controlled substances," the doctor told him. "The lab's never seen anything like it."

He might not have had HIV, but his body thought he did. While Ozzy was relieved to hear he didn't have the virus, the doctor told him that the life he was living was causing him to suffer from the functional equivalent of HIV, and he was still in jeopardy.

"Mr. Osbourne, you might not be HIV positive, but your life is still in grave danger if you don't take it easier," the doctor cautioned him. That last bit of advice went in one ear and out the other, and at the time, he changed nothing about his lifestyle and kept drinking and taking drugs. He did, however, say that the scare had made him finally stop cheating on his wife, so it was a teachable moment at least.

Ozzy apppears to forget his worries onstage at New Jersey's Meadowlands Arena in 1988.

38

NO REST FOR THE WICKED

OZZY SETS ON A NEW COURSE WITH ZAKK WYLDE

SEPTEMBER 28, 1988

Ozzy and guitarist Zakk Wylde bring wanton heavy metal butchery to East Rutherford, New Jersey in 1988.

ZZ Top. There's a *lot* of southern rock in his playing, which is pretty unexpected for an Ozzy record. His inventiveness creates an unpredictability that keeps the proceedings interesting.

"Breaking All the Rules" is another song that benefits from Wylde's approach. The rhythm guitar is tuned down, and the leads offer a combination of the required shredding and some blues phrases thrown in to keep listeners guessing. "Tattooed Dancer," a comparatively short track buried in the middle of side two, also features some great work by Wylde.

There are, sadly, some duds on the record too. There is no key Wylde can tune down to, no number of pinched harmonics, that could turn "Bloodbath in Paradise" into anything but an incredibly stupid song about the Manson Family. And while Osbourne is to be commended for his candor in the lyrics to the song "Demon Alcohol," it's kind of hard to understand what effect he was going for with the music, which strangely recalls King's X in parts. Again, Zakk Wylde does most of the work here.

The album ends on a lyrically and musically upbeat note with "Hero." While the record is not perfect, it shows Osbourne being a little more excited and involved, and the music shows him looking forward and chasing new ideas. Zakk Wylde is a significant source of those new ideas, and just like a post-Sabbath Ozzy was reinvigorated when he found Randy Rhoads, an Ozzy who had been floundering somewhat creatively on the last two albums seems to find his footing here. It has its weaknesses, but it's his best studio album since *Diary of a Madman*, and it positioned him well for the coming decade.

Released in 1988, *No Rest for the Wicked* shows Ozzy Osbourne in a somewhat better light than he was in for the two previous albums. A big reason for that is guitarist Zakk Wylde, who makes his debut here.

Osbourne is a musician who needs a guitarist to act as a foil for him. As skilled as Jake E. Lee was, that partnership wasn't really a Love Connection, as far as the music they produced was concerned. Right off the bat, when *No Rest for the Wicked* kicks off with the song "Miracle Man," it's clear that Osbourne's partnership with Wylde is a good one.

"Miracle Man" is that most late-80s of creatures, the anti-televangelist metal song. At that time, American television preachers like Jimmy Swaggart and Jim Bakker were being revealed as huge hypocrites whose entire anti-metal stance was wholly contrived to extract donations from gullible parishioners. Since metal bands bore the brunt of their criticism, they were only too happy to pile on. It got old quickly, but the gloating was fun for a week or so.

No Rest for the Wicked suffers from a lot of the same problems as its predecessors in terms of production, but the poppiness is dialed back a couple of notches, in part thanks to Zakk Wylde's guitar playing, which is just too attention-getting to fade politely into the background. On the single "Crazy Babies," Wylde throws in some almost bluesy guitar that sounds like a bottleneck slide and recalls early

39

OZZY LOSES HIS DAMN MIND

REACHING A NEW NADIR

SEPTEMBER 3, 1989

Why Ozzy, we didn't know you drank!

Ozzy Osbourne said in his memoir that he found out he had almost fatally strangled his wife in a way that was entirely on-brand for him in the 1980s. He woke up in jail after an alcoholic blackout and was told what he had done by a police officer outside of his holding cell.

"John Michael Osbourne, you are hereby charged with the attempted murder by strangulation of your wife, Sharon Osbourne, during a domestic disturbance that took place in the early hours of Sunday, September 3, 1989, at Beel House, Little Chalfont, in the county of Buckinghamshire," the officer informed him.

The incident ironically had its genesis at 1989's Moscow Music Peace Festival. Sharon Osbourne told the *Guardian* in 2001 that he had come back from the performance, imbibed four bottles of vodka, then told her, "I've decided you have to go," and tried to strangle her. According to his memoir, he was naked when this happened.

Sharon called the police, her husband got picked up, and he ended up doing a months-long stint in rehab. When she spoke to the *Guardian* about the incident, she said that it shouldn't have been too surprising that he would engage in behavior like that in his state.

"He was totally insane from all the drink and drugs he was doing, and well, these things happen," she said.

Osbourne said that after his court appearance, as he was being driven to rehab, the car he was in passed a newspaper kiosk, which was festooned with publications proclaiming what the singer had done in giant, bold-faced type, such as "DEATH THREAT OZZY SENT TO BOOZE CLINIC." He was there for a few months by his own account before his wife came to visit him, and when she did, he was sure she would hand him divorce papers. Instead, she said she was dropping the charges against him. He asked the question that many people probably asked upon hearing that she was staying with him—why?

"I don't believe you're capable of attempted murder, Ozzy," she explained. "It's not in you. You're a sweet, gentle man. But when you get drunk, Ozzy Osbourne disappears, and someone else takes over. I want that other person to go away, Ozzy. I don't want to see him again. *Ever*."

Spoiler Alert: She would see drunk Ozzy again, and she would see him more than once. But while he never again tried to murder her, she did give him points for keeping it real. "I see that Eminem gets in trouble for singing about killing his wife," she told the *Guardian*. "At least my husband actually tried to do it!"

Ozzy performs at the Moscow Music Festival on August 12, 1989. The concert featured various bands and was held to raise money to combat drug abuse, natch.

PART 4

RETIREMENT SUCKS, 1990–1998

Ozzy poses with guitarist Zakk Wylde in Japan in 1989. Thank god they remembered the crimping iron.

40

JUST SAY OZZY

AN ABOVE-AVERAGE LIVE SOUVENIR

MARCH 17, 1990

Ozzy at the heavy metal music industry convention known as the Foundations Forum in Los Angeles in 1990.

Gather 'round, kids, gather 'round. Grandpa Bukszpan is here to explain to all of you young 'uns what a "stopgap measure" is as it pertained to the music industry circa 1990.

In the twentieth century, musical artists were expected to churn out an album every year. If they couldn't, the record company would panic because going a year without a new release was commercial suicide. Frequently, the solution to this terrible problem was to throw a live album out there, lest the kids forget you exist.

Just Say Ozzy was just such a measure. This live EP comes in at a tidy thirty minutes and features just six songs, which the liner notes say were recorded in London at Brixton Academy in November 1989. Since its release, there has been great speculation that it was actually a studio recording or that at least some of it was live, and the rest was recorded in the studio, with applause added later.

Whatever the case, this allegedly live stopgap measure shows Ozzy in good

form. The band consists of Zakk Wylde on guitar, the late Randy Castillo on drums, and former Black Sabbath bassist Geezer Butler holding down the low end.

To the band's credit, the live versions of Ozzy's solo tracks fare better than their original studio counterparts. "Miracle Man," "Bloodbath in Paradise," and "Tattooed Dancer" are much better than the *No Rest for the Wicked* versions, and no less an authority than Ozzy himself proclaimed the recording of "Shot in the Dark" found here to be his favorite.

After those four songs, the band performs Black Sabbath's "Sweet Leaf" and "War Pigs." Neither version comes anywhere close to dethroning the originals, but if you can ignore Castillo's overly busy drum fills and Wylde's compulsive need to perform a pinch-harmonic every five seconds, they're pretty good. Even if their trademark instrument noises eventually wear out their welcome, these musicians could really play.

Just Say Ozzy was out of print for years and was eventually reissued as part

of the *See You on the Other Side* vinyl box set in 2019. Part of what kept it off record store shelves was a dispute over the songwriting credits for "Shot in the Dark," which bassist Phil Soussan brought to Osbourne when he joined the band for 1986's *The Ultimate Sin*. The song was based on another track that he had co-written with his previous band, Wildlife, and the issue of the songwriting credits was instrumental in keeping several albums out of print as the dispute went on. That includes this one.

Just Say Ozzy may not be an absolutely essential part of the Ozzy Osbourne catalog, but it's a fine addition, and getting to hear the solo material performed with a little more *oomph* and a less intrusive mix is a marked improvement. Hopefully, the legal shenanigans and disputes regarding *Just Say Ozzy* will be resolved so everyone can hear it without illegally downloading it from some dodgy Russian torrent site that puts twenty viruses on your computer.

41

NO MORE TEARS

OZZY'S FIRST FULL-LENGTH OF THE 90s

SEPTEMBER 17, 1991

1991's *No More Tears* was the second studio album Ozzy Osbourne made with guitarist Zakk Wylde and his first of the 1990s. It features the same lineup as *No Rest for the Wicked*—Wylde, drummer Randy Castillo, and bassist Bob Daisley—and here, they sound more like a coherent band than they did on *No Rest for the Wicked*, which sounded much more like a bunch of guys who didn't know each other, individually overdubbing their parts on separate days in the studio.

As was the case on *No Rest for the Wicked*, Wylde does a lot of the heavy lifting here. His guitar style had always borrowed a dash of blues or country as a decorative flourish, but here it's his full-fledged style, leading "I Don't Want to Change the World" to get a guitar solo that wouldn't sound totally out of place on a Molly Hatchet album. That approach permeates his style throughout, and it gives most of the record a fresh and unexpected sound that closed the book on the 1980s and showed a way forward for the coming decade.

The album's release couldn't possibly have been timed any better. It came out one month after Metallica's self-titled album created a favorable environment for the heavy stuff and one week before Nirvana's *Nevermind* came along and upended the entire musical landscape.

Somehow, Ozzy had managed to plant a flag at precisely the right time because *No More Tears* went on to sell millions of copies while almost every other artist associated with 80s heavy metal stood by helplessly and saw their fortunes plummet.

Regardless of what was going on in the popular culture at the time, *No More Tears* would not have sold millions of copies if people didn't like it, and there are many reasons to like it. The material is strong for the most part, the production still glistens but doesn't interfere, and the performances are all somewhere on the good-to-great spectrum. The title track, in particular, is a compelling mix of heavy crunch, Sabbath-flavored vocal melodies, and a highly addictive descending riff on the choruses. The only problem is the song's mid-section, when the crunchy plodding is interrupted by an instrumental break that seems utterly unnecessary and grafted in from some other song.

Ultimately, *No More Tears* adds up to an entertaining listen that rarely bores. It gave Osbourne the popularity to continue into the 1990s, and you can even hear a little bit of Black Label Society in some of the guitar riffs and leads, so it was a good gig for Zakk Wylde too.

The coming decade would see popular music take a lot of stylistic twists and turns, and *No More Tears* showed that Ozzy and company would be able to weather them. Luckily, grunge ended just a couple of years later, and Osbourne had never fooled with it in an attempt at popularity, so he gets the last laugh.

Ozzy gets a few things off his chest
in Chicago, November 1991.

42

OZZY RETIRES, VOLUME I

THE SINGER PROCLAIMS HIS 1992 TOUR TO BE HIS LAST

NOVEMBER 15, 1992

In his memoir, Ozzy Osbourne said that his health began to decline after the release of *No More Tears*. Initially, he chalked it up to years of substance abuse, but the symptoms he was experiencing were new and indicated that something more serious may have been happening.

"I started to notice a tremor in my hand," he wrote. "My speech was slurred. I was always exhausted."

A specialist in Boston ran a battery of tests. While he couldn't diagnose Osbourne with a particular disease, he said that the singer was experiencing symptoms that might indicate either multiple sclerosis or Parkinson's disease. The specialist couldn't be sure, so Ozzy went to another doctor for a second opinion. That doctor said the same thing—these symptoms might be multiple sclerosis or Parkinson's disease, but there wasn't enough evidence to convict.

"Aside from your drug addiction and your alcoholism, you're a very healthy man, Mr. Osbourne," the second doctor told him. "My considered medical opinion is that you should leave my office and go and live your life."

Rather than interpret the doctor's statement as a license to keep snorting live ants, Osbourne decided it meant it was time to retire. Hearing the terms "multiple sclerosis" and "Parkinson's disease" had scared the crap out of him, and after surviving twenty-five years of heavy metal excess, maybe it was time to stop. He had unquestionably accomplished more than most people do in five lifetimes, and the fact that he was still here to tell the tale meant that he would be quitting while he was ahead.

Osbourne embarked on the "No More Tours" North American tour to commemorate the occasion, which lasted from June 9 to November 15 of 1992. Interestingly, the choice of opening acts said a lot about the state of popular music at the time. When the tour started, the openers included Faster Pussycat and Slaughter. When it ended, Alice in Chains did the honors—it was a case study in the death of glam and the birth of grunge.

The tour was not without its drama. On its final night, the original Black Sabbath lineup was to reunite for four songs, and at the time, Black Sabbath was on tour with singer Ronnie James Dio. Dio had replaced Ozzy in 1979 then left in 1982 to pursue a solo career after an acrimonious split. He returned in 1991 and made a new album and toured with them, but he refused to go along with the idea of opening up for the guy he had replaced.

Rob Halford of Judas Priest was drafted to front Black Sabbath on the final night before the reunion performance. Both sets—with Halford fronting the band and then Ozzy doing the honors—have been heavily bootlegged, with many copies of said bootleg proclaiming the night to be one that would live forever in heavy metal history. That's debatable, but Halford deserves credit for saving the day at the last minute, even if the first thing he did that night was come in too early on "Children of the Grave."

Ozzy and Zakk Wylde bring both the pain and the dry ice to Brixton Academy in 1992.

43

LIVE & LOUD

OZZY'S FINAL ALBUM UNTIL THE NEXT ONE

JUNE 28, 1993

Ozzy guitarist and right-hand man Zakk Wylde showers Brixton Academy with pinch-harmonics and Lynyrd Skynyrd licks in 1992.

Live & Loud was intended to be a souvenir for fans from Ozzy Osbourne's farewell party. His "No More Tours" tour was over, and he intended to disappear forever into the swirling and unforgiving eddy known as rock 'n' roll retirement. As a final keepsake of Ozzy the Touring Entity, *Live & Loud* was intended to be the grand and fitting send-off that spanned his entire career, and it would have been if he had actually managed to stay retired. He was, of course, unable to, but the fact remains that if this had been the last thing he ever released, few people could complain.

The songs were almost all performed in August 1992 as the "No More Tours" outing was coming to a close. The band on this collection is the same as the one on *No More Tears*, except for bassist Mike Inez, who took the place of the departed Bob Daisley. The only exception is "Black Sabbath," which was performed by the original lineup of Black Sabbath on the last night of the tour.

While Osbourne has seen his share of musicians come and go, the band on this collection sounds like a real band, with interplay and everything. It would not be an exaggeration to say that Zakk Wylde once again plays his ass off— indeed, he plays like a man possessed, a man trying to singlehandedly deliver the entire show himself. Luckily, Inez and drummer Randy Castillo are up to the challenge, and they all play well off of each other. There is no weak link here.

The best performances tend to be songs like "Mr. Crowley" and "Crazy Train," which originate from *Blizzard of Ozz*. The band may have performed these songs a bunch of times before it was recorded for *Live & Loud*, but their excitement while performing those songs is palpable.

Inez and Wylde are both Gen Xers, so they would have been teenagers when that album came out, and they play the songs like fans performing the music

of their idols. During "I Don't Know," it's very easy to imagine a mullet-sporting teenaged Zakk Wylde listening to the song over and over again and poring over the liner notes as the record spins, resolving to practice his guitar every night for as long as it took to be as good as this Randy Rhoads guy.

The album draws to a close with the reunited original members of Black Sabbath performing their namesake song. It's a good performance, but one gets the sense from listening to it that it was more about getting the original members together on stage for posterity than trying to beat the original recording.

It's followed by "Changes," which is performed by Ozzy on vocals, Zakk Wylde

on piano, and an army of synthesized violins. With that, the album comes to a close, and if you were paying attention at the time, Ozzy's career was supposedly finished too. Of course, if you were paying attention, you didn't believe it for a minute anyway, so when the singer announced his triumphant return, you were not surprised. Still, if this had been the last thing he ever did, as he had initially intended it to be, it would have put a period on his career in fine fashion.

44

THE "RETIREMENT SUCKS" TOUR

HE LEFT. HE DID NOTHING. HE CAME BACK.

JUNE 9, 1995

Let's say, for argument's sake, that being a professional musician was the only thing you had ever done in your entire life with any kind of stability. Let's say further that it was, in fact, the only paying gig you'd ever had that you actually enjoyed. In those circumstances, stopping is probably really hard. Your body may not be able to do things it could do when you were a mere lad of twenty-one, but your mind doesn't care. It will insist that you resume the activity you have resolved to put to the side, human frailty and the aging process be damned.

This is the pickle in which Ozzy Osbourne found himself after coming off the road in 1992. Sure, now he had time to become a Walmart greeter or a museum docent, but those vocations didn't play to his strengths. He was Ozzy Goddamn Osbourne, the Prince of Darkness, and he belonged on the concert stage.

He certainly had reasons to stay retired. In his memoir, he said that getting off the road had improved his health "dramatically," to the point where he wasn't even living in fear of multiple sclerosis or Parkinson's disease anymore. However, as soon as his health had improved, he was overcome with the condition that retirement could never defeat—boredom. And with that, he announced that he would return to the concert stage with the "Retirement Sucks" tour.

The tour began on June 9, 1995, in Nottingham with a setlist that leaned heavily on the eternal classics, such as "Mr. Crowley," "Crazy Train," and "Paranoid." It wound its way through North and South America, the United Kingdom, and Europe before its final date on Halloween 1996 in Anchorage, Alaska. All told, the tour consisted of eighty-eight dates, more than enough for the singer to decide whether or not retirement truly sucked.

According to *Billboard*, the tour was one of the Top 10 highest-grossing tours of

1996, right up there with the original reunited lineup of KISS, Jimmy Buffett of "Cheeseburger in Paradise" fame, and the reunited Eagles, whose "Hell Freezes Over" tour caused many onlookers to conclude that retirement sucked for the Eagles too, due to the notable absence of any tequila sunrises or witchy women.

Billboard tried to be kind in describing the Ozzy Osbourne concert experience circa 1996. The publication did not come out and say he sounded terrible, but their description of his performance suggested he wasn't all the way back to his fighting weight just yet.

"Four years after announcing his retirement, Ozzy Osbourne went out on the road for a tour named 'Retirement Sucks,'" it said. "What he may have lacked vocally, he made up for visually, with a

Ozzy gets airborne at Monsters of Rock at Donington in 1996.

OZZY MEET & GREET

humorous video of himself superimposed over various celebrities including Elvis and Madonna."

Sadly, it wasn't just *Billboard*. Many reviews of the tour said that Osbourne's voice, which was never the world's greatest technical marvel in the first place, had suffered from four years of inactivity. Don De Leaumont of the metal blog *Southeast of Heaven* described seeing the man himself on May 18, 1996, in Atlanta, and the news was not great.

"It was totally obvious that his voice was shot," De Leaumont recalled. "I really wish I could say that this was a great memory for me but instead, it's a show I wish never would have happened."

Ouch. Apparently, sometimes, retirement isn't the only thing that sucks.

OZZY SUPPORT

OZZY PHOTO / MEDIA

45

OZZMOSIS

Ozzy in 1995 at the pyramids of Teotihuacan in Mexico City. Do they sell that groovy vest at the gift shop?

OZZY GETS AS 90s AS *FRIENDS* AND FLANNEL

OCTOBER 23, 1995

The 1990s were a famously trying time for rock musicians, particularly those heavily identified with the previous decade. Perhaps conscious of this state of affairs, Ozzy Osbourne chose Michael Bienhorn to produce his next album, *Ozzmosis*. Bienhorn had produced albums by such acts as the Red Hot Chili Peppers, Soul Asylum, and Soundgarden, and he was there to get a "modern" sound for Ozzy's new album, or at least "modern" by 1995 standards.

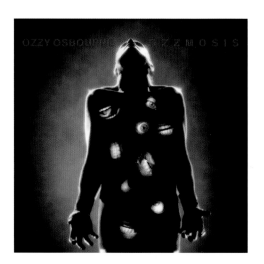

To an extent, the gambit worked, which isn't something you can say for every rock artist who tried to stay relevant in the 90s. The opener, "Perry Mason," is a solid headbanger provided you can successfully ignore the incredibly stupid lyrics. "I Just Want You" is also perfectly serviceable, provided you can successfully ignore the very average vocal melody and chord progression.

"Ghost Behind My Eyes" is one of the songs that shows the most 90s influence, recalling Soundgarden and Type O Negative at several points. It's followed by "Thunder Underground," which has some residual Sabbath DNA and features some of Ozzy's highest-pitched vocals since "Sabbath Bloody Sabbath."

Now, we have to talk about "See You on the Other Side."

To the extent that the album keeps it together for the first four songs, it all falls apart here. A ballad co-written by Motörhead's Lemmy Kilmister, it goes on *forever*, despite a listed running time of only six minutes and ten seconds. If that's actually true, and it's really only that long, then congratulations are due to Ozzy and company for unlocking the secret to stretching the perception of time with a single piece of music.

"Tomorrow," luckily, is much better. It's a midtempo rocker in which the band just kind of performs the song without trying to wow the listener with how "current" it sounds. Zakk Wylde, as always, plays like a demon, even when the material around him seems less than inspiring. He particularly distinguishes himself on "Denial," peppering the listener with flurries of manic notes like former Vice President Dick Cheney spraying Harry Whittington's face with birdshot shrapnel.

Ironically, much of the criticism of this album at the time singled it out for lack of stylistic progress from those that had preceded it. In fact, critic Chuck Eddy wrote in *Entertainment Weekly* that "Ghost Behind My Eyes" is the "most tolerable" outing on the album due only to its sappiness.

The album wraps up with "Old L.A. Tonight," an above-average ballad that isn't a bad

way to go out. It just goes on for a really long time. In general, the main criticism of this record is the length of the songs. Everything goes on for longer than it needs to, and it really doesn't help much. "My Jekyll Doesn't Hide," for example, has all the makings of an excellent three-minute song. It goes on for six minutes.

Generally, everything on *Ozzmosis* has an unfortunate tendency to drag like

that, which is a shame because there's some good stuff here that could have been edited down by a brutal gardener of a producer to a tidy forty minutes or so. On the plus side, it seems to go on for less time than *St. Anger*, so *yay*?

46

OZZAPALOOZA

OZZFEST IS BORN,
HILARITY ENSUES

OCTOBER 25, 1996

Ozzy inaugurates the mother of all heavy metal
festivals in San Bernardino on the first Ozzfest tour.

In Ozzy's memoir, he fondly recalled the moment when he decided he had had enough of being retired in the aftermath of "No More Tours." He said that he asked Sharon to get him a gig at "one of those American festivals," which got the ball rolling.

While that was the catalyst for his return, it was not without some pain. Sharon contacted the organizers of Lollapalooza, which had turned from a one-time tour to mark the retirement of Jane's Addiction into an annual event. Clearly, the Lollapalooza organizers must have thought retirement sucked too and would welcome the returning Ozzy with open arms.

Unfortunately, any feelings of sympathy with one another's predicaments ended with that phone call. The Lollapalooza organizers told Sharon that their festival was fresh and new, Ozzy was old and musty, and maybe some Six Flags amusement park somewhere would book him. Come back when you're Moby. We don't want you.

Rather than bow and scrape until the Lollapalooza organizers let Ozzy take a noon slot on the second stage, Sharon decided that they should just put on their own festival instead. It would be called "Ozzfest," a name whose similarity

to "Beerfest" amused Ozzy to no end. However, he kept his thoughts to himself about its similarity to Oktoberfest or QuiltFest.

Like Lollapalooza, Ozzfest was initially conceived as a one-time thing. It took place on October 25 and 26, 1996, in Phoenix on the first day and in Devore, California, the next day. Whoever chose the bands who performed had clearly been paying attention to the state of metal at the time, as the roster boasted Slayer, Danzig, Biohazard, and Fear Factory, among others. Ozzy wrote in his memoir that the lineup was like this very much by design.

"Our strategy was to take all the undesirables, all the bands that couldn't find an outlet anywhere else, and put them together, give them an audience," he wrote. He said this was necessary because the state of the music business at the time was outright hostile to new bands, and he wanted them to have the same chance to build themselves up that he and his fellow travelers in Black Sabbath had.

"It had got to the point in the music business where if you wanted to play a gig, the venues made you buy all the tickets in advance, so you had to give

them away for free or sell them on your own, which is bullshit," he wrote. "Black Sabbath never had to deal with that kind of bollocks in the early days. We'd never have left Aston."

Ozzfest became a massive success, and just like Lollapalooza, it became an annual event that toured the world. That changed in the 2010s when there were a few years in which it didn't take place, and the last Ozzfest-branded event took place in 2018. At the same time, the festival went to some pretty far-flung places that many other big festivals skip, such as Poland, the Czech Republic, Israel, and Japan.

Ozzfest was also the catalyst for another big event that many people had been hoping for. Ozzy wrote in his memoir that after the success of the first festival, Sharon suggested that 1997's Ozzfest should be headlined by the original lineup of Black Sabbath. Ozzy agreed, and it was time to start making awkward phone calls.

47

BLACK SABBATH REUNITES, VOLUME I

EVERYTHING OLD IS NEW AGAIN

DECEMBER 4, 1997

Ozzy performs at his namesake festival Ozzfest in
1997 at Giants Stadium.

When Ozzy's camp reached out to Black Sabbath guitarist Tony Iommi to discuss a reunion of the original lineup, the singer was negotiating from a position of strength. Iommi was not.

By the 1990s, the Black Sabbath name was only meaningful to the most committed diehard fans. To everyone else, it had become a name from the distant past that now meant "Tony Iommi and a revolving door of sidemen." The band had seen some truly legendary musicians in its ranks post-Ozzy, including Glenn Hughes of Deep Purple and Cozy Powell of Rainbow. Unfortunately, the constant instability in the lineup gave a lot of fans the impression that the band was just kind of a disorganized shitshow and not worth bothering with.

Even though Ozzy's career had over-shadowed that of his former band, he still harbored hurt feelings over his 1979 firing. So when Ozzy and Iommi reconnected to discuss a possible reunion, the singer asked why it had happened, even though the event was almost twenty years in the past. Iommi cited Osbourne's drinking as a significant factor, and while that wasn't exactly news to the singer, he said that hearing it this time, it sunk in.

That summer, the original lineup went out on the road. They did so without drummer Bill Ward, who was suffering from various health issues, and had Faith No More's Mike Bordin filling in for him. However, by December 1997, he was back on the drum throne for two shows performed and recorded at Birmingham National Exhibition Centre, fittingly enough. Osbourne described the two shows in his memoir as "fucking phenomenal."

"Even though I've always played Sabbath songs on stage, it's never as good as when the four of us do them," he wrote.

In addition to the reunion tour, the band had also intended to make a new studio album, their first together since 1978's *Never Say Die!* They got two songs recorded—"Psycho Man" and "Selling My Soul"—but before they could get any further, Ward had a major heart attack at the recording studio and had to be taken away in an ambulance.

Ward's health eventually recovered enough for him to come back to the band, but it had taken quite some time, and by then, whatever momentum there had been at the beginning of the sessions was gone. And with that, the first album featuring the reunited original Black Sabbath lineup fell by the wayside.

Osbourne wrote in his memoir that the press had blamed the failure to turn out a new studio album on his "ego." In reality, he said it didn't work out because of something a lot less controversial—they were all twenty years older now, they had all changed, and the way things used to work in the old days wasn't how things worked now. Osbourne had been a solo act now for twice as long as he had been a member of Sabbath, after all, and the situation was no longer the same.

The band salvaged their work as best they could, releasing the *Reunion* album, which was taken from recordings of their Birmingham concerts and included the two studio tracks. Fans had hoped for a lot more, but this would have to do for now.

48

BLACK SABBATH— *REUNION*

SAVAGE LIVE RECORDINGS MAKE THIS ONE WORTHWHILE

OCTOBER 20, 1998

Culled from the recordings of the first reunion of Black Sabbath's original lineup in 1997, *Reunion* is a potent reminder of what a beast this band was. Osbourne wrote in his memoir that what you hear on the album is exactly what the audience heard those two nights. There were no overdubs, no fancy stuff, just four dudes pushing fifty who were still capable of playing like their lives depended on it.

The performances are not perfect, and flubs and clams can be heard throughout. It doesn't matter at all. The original lineup never executed things flawlessly—they were about sheer brutality and pummeling, which is what you hear for the entire live portion of this album.

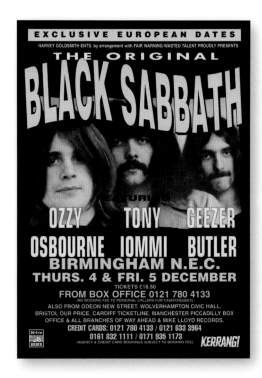

It's almost like no time had passed since the original disbandment, and the group is still the same barbarian entity that it was when every member was twenty-one. All of the interplay is there, all of the swing is there, and the only significant difference is that Osbourne is a more confident frontman.

The set leans very heavily on the first four studio albums, and except for "Dirty Women" from *Technical Ecstasy*, their final three are not represented at all. No one in the audience seems to care. You will not hear a single ticket holder cry out to hear "Swinging the Chain."

The two studio songs that the band managed to record before Bill Ward's heart attack, "Psycho Man" and "Selling My Soul," round out the set. While neither song will ever be "Paranoid" or "Iron Man," they're both a lot better than any of us had any right to expect from these guys at this point in their careers.

If there's any complaint to be had, it's that the band sounds less like four equals and more like solo Ozzy using the others as a very tight backing band. That's not a knock, either—Tony, Geezer, and Bill all bring their "A" game to the proceedings and play as well as ever. But after twenty

years as a successful solo act, you just couldn't expect Ozzy to be anyone but "successful solo act Ozzy Osbourne" at that point.

The live stuff on the album is worth the purchase price, but it's really a shame that the band couldn't finish the studio tracks. Based on just the two that were made, this iteration of the band seemed to be excited to be back together and creating again, and also seemed to be happy to put behind them the pain and hurt feelings that had resulted from Osbourne's firing.

Luckily, the story didn't end there. Black Sabbath would reunite in the future for more tours and recording. The sad part is that this was likely the last, best chance for all four original members to make another album together, and it didn't happen. Black Sabbath would go on to make a full studio album and embark on triumphant world tours, but original drummer Bill Ward would not be a part of it. However you slice it, that sucks.

Tony Iommi performs with Black Sabbath's original lineup in Birmingham in 1997. Is he actually *smiling*?

THE ORIGINAL
BLACK SABBATH
HOME AT LAST
DEC. 4 & 5 1997
BIRMINGHAM N.E.C.

PART 5

"SHAAAARON!!!", 2001—2007

We're a happy family. Kelly, Sharon, Jack, and Ozzy in 2003.

49

DOWN TO EARTH

OZZY'S FIRST SOLO ALBUM OF THE 9/11 ERA

OCTOBER 16, 2001

When Ozzy came to America in 2001, he came wrapped in the flag and (one assumes) carrying a cross.

A month after the terrorist attacks of September 11, 2001, Ozzy Osbourne released his eighth solo studio album, *Down to Earth*. It had been six years since *Ozzmosis*, and between that, Ozzfest, and the Black Sabbath reunion, a lot had happened. Would the new album reflect all that had gone on in a fascinating new light, or would it just be an exercise in repetitive, warmed-over bullshit?

The lineup on this album is Zakk Wylde on guitar, Robert Trujillo on bass, and Mike Bordin on drums. It starts off very promisingly with "Gets Me Through," a song dedicated to the singer's fans. Rather than opening the album with a straight rager, the track starts the album out quietly and builds, with Osbourne assuring us all that he's "not the antichrist or the Iron Man."

On the second track, the chugging rocker "Facing Hell," the musicians serve him well and provide as solid a backing band as you could ask for. Then, you have "Dreamer," a sappy environmental ballad co-written by Mick Jones of Foreigner. It was released as a single and charted well, but in the context of the album, it just kind of slows things down. Thankfully, Zakk Wylde seems to have no problem soloing over a power ballad and getting his Don Felder on, redeeming what would have been a real filler track otherwise.

"No Easy Way Out" is another midtempo rocker that's well-served by Zakk Wylde's guitar playing and gets into a few textures that wouldn't be out of place on a middle-period Queen album. While the decision to use outside songwriters like Marti Frederiksen may have caused some side-eye—he did pen hits for Carrie Underwood and Faith Hill, after all—he gets results, and the songwriting on *Down to Earth* is generally better than that of its last couple of predecessors.

Strangely, the attempts at straight-forward rock, like "That I Never Had," don't fare very well, even though this kind of

music is what Ozzy is famous for. In many cases, it's the more artistically risky stuff that fares better than the meat-and-potatoes material. Maybe if "That I Never Had" was based on a decent riff or discernable melody, it might have been an improvement, but you can almost hear producer Tim Palmer trying to make Wylde meet a "chugga chugga" quota before he can go home for the night.

"You Know . . . (Part 1)" starts off in ballad territory, but it thankfully lasts for only a minute before the whole band kicks in for "Junkie." In case you couldn't tell from the title, the song is about addiction, and you definitely get the feeling from listening to it that Ozzy knows a thing or two about the subject. Wylde also pulls some interesting sounds out of his guitar and should be commended for trying some new tricks.

"Running Out of Time" is another ballad co-written by Foreigner's Mick Jones, and at this point, it's safe to say that he's the least valuable player on the record. Sure, rock singers need ballads if they want to climb the charts, but Jones's songs on this album are simply not good. So the minute you hear those opening piano notes, please avail yourself of the "skip" button on your playback device of choice. That's free advice.

Despite the balladry and a few other questionable choices, *Down to Earth* is overall a solid album and makes the case that even thirty years into his career, the singer still had lots to offer. The album itself sold well and positioned Osbourne well for the new millennium, and while it's no *Blizzard of Ozz*, it's an entertaining listen with enjoyable songs.

LIVE AT BUDOKAN

A LIVE SET THAT LEANS HEAVILY ON THE CLASSICS

FEBRUARY 15, 2002

Recorded on one night at the legendary Nippon Budokan in Tokyo, *Live at Budokan* shows Ozzy in good voice and his band in good form. Backed by the same Wylde-Trujillo-Bordin lineup that had supported him on *Down to Earth* and bolstered by the presence of keyboard player John Sinclair, the thirteen-song CD was released with a companion DVD.

The CD only features three songs from *Down to Earth*—"That I Never Had," "Junkie," and "Gets Me Through." The rest is songs from *No More Tears*, Ozzy's 80s output, and an encore of "Paranoid." Omitted from the CD but present on the DVD is "Suicide Solution," which is also attached to Zakk Wylde's solo guitar turn.

On the DVD, that whole bit goes on for thirteen minutes. Arguably, it could have been added to the CD, which clocks in at sixty-six minutes and could have accommodated it. But perhaps cooler heads prevailed. The unaccompanied solo is something better seen than heard and if you've ever suffered through all of "The Mule" on Deep Purple's *Made in Japan*, you know this to be the case.

The performances are strong overall, and despite Osbourne's history of live recordings that need a little post-production spit and polish, this one is comparatively raw and doesn't show many signs of studio wizardry. Obviously there's got to be *some* after-the-fact surgery, but Osbourne is to be commended for turning in a live

performance that didn't need a month in the studio afterward to salvage.

Once again, the band pulls out all the stops here and gives Ozzy a solid foundation to work over. Zakk Wylde again plays like a complete maniac. While he sometimes goes overboard with the extraterrestrial noises and intermittent harmonic shrieks, you can tell that he's having the time of his life up there, alternating between faithful, note-perfect executions of Randy Rhoads licks and moments where he goes completely off-book. On previous live recordings, he played like a Randy Rhoads fan engaging in the act of tribute. On *Live at Budokan*, he's long since come into his own and makes his own mark.

As good a recording as it is, some might wonder if doing a live album at this point was 100 percent necessary. The previous one, *Live & Loud*, was not even ten years in the past, and only two studio albums had come out since then, one of which is not represented on this recording at all. Having said that, it's a good album with solid performances and one of the only rock albums recorded in Japan in which the crowd actually seems to get pretty rowdy.

Live at Budokan may not be the most necessary album in the Ozzy Osbourne catalog, but completist fans will undoubtedly want it, and even Ozzy hobbyists will probably like it. *Live & Loud* remains the best live Ozzy album to date, but this one is no slouch and is more than worth sixty-six minutes of your time.

Ozzy makes the same mistake so many made before him of going full Lestat. Never go full Lestat.

51

THE OSBOURNES ON MTV

THE WORLD'S FAVORITE DOVE-DECAPITATING DAD

MARCH 5, 2002

Ozzy and Sharon with their very happy children Jack and Kelly at home (otherwise known as the set of the reality show *The Osbournes*) in 2002.

Though many may not have realized it at the time, a new reality show that premiered on MTV in March of 2002 would become the highest-rated show ever in the network's history. That show was *The Osbournes*, and it depicted the day-to-day mayhem that took place in the home of the singer, his wife and manager, Sharon, and their kids, Jack and Kelly.

Because every member of the Osbourne family says the word "fuck" over and over again, the show was heavily bleeped when it aired on television. If anything, it became as synonymous with constant bleeping noises as it was with the singer yelling "Shaaaaaaron!!!!" and their daughter Kelly looking constantly horrified.

There was almost no story to speak of, but viewers didn't care. It was a wall-to-wall freak show. It featured things like Sharon throwing an entire ham over the wall into their adjoining neighbor's yard, Ozzy revealing the extent of his Viagra use, and of course, the moment when he rejects Sharon's attempt to use bubbles at one of his concerts as a visual effect because he's "the Prince of Fucking Darkness."

Whatever the family's expectations for the show might have been, it was an instant hit, and it made the singer and his family the most unlikely of celebrities. Indeed, Ozzy said it made his entire family famous, even among people who never cared for his music.

"I was walking around Manhattan and people who wouldn't generally come up to me were going: 'It's them—it's Sharon and Ozzy Osbourne,'" he told Biography.com. "We broadened our audience by millions."

Their eldest child, Aimee, did not participate in the show or appear with the family during promotional appearances. In 2008, she told *the Independent* that this was because she had her own musical aspirations and didn't think the show would do her any favors.

"I want to be a singer, and I felt if I'd stayed with the Osbournes and done the whole thing I would have been typecast right away," she said, adding that she wasn't remotely interested in having her personal business broadcast to an audience of millions. "I'm more reserved and my private life is very important."

Though the highly rated show could probably have gone on for decades, it lasted only three seasons, and the family incurred some damage during that time.

In 2009, the singer told Kate Thornton of BBC Radio 2's *Line of Enquiry* that he was utterly intoxicated for all three seasons of the show.

"When the filming ended, I'd go in my little bunker and smoke a pipe and drink about a case of beer every day . . . I used to do a lot of prescription drugs as well," he revealed. Sharon co-signed, saying he "wasn't sober for one day."

Fun Fact: Despite the show's massive success, attempts to revive it were less successful. In March 2009, the first episode of the variety show *Osbournes: Reloaded* aired on Fox to unanimous critical hostility. Roger Catlin of the *Hartford Courant* proclaimed it the "worst variety show ever," which is quite a claim if you've ever seen *The Starland Vocal Band Show* or that *Brady Bunch* atrocity with Geri Reischl as fake Jan. But what really killed *Osbournes: Reloaded* was the network itself. According to *The Wrap*, 14 percent of Fox affiliates refused to air it due to "content concerns."

52

BLIZZARD OF OVERDUBS

OZZY'S ORIGINAL RHYTHM SECTION EVAPORATES

APRIL 2, 2002

As George Lucas learned when he made Greedo shoot first, you can't mess around with a classic. Or you can, but you can expect people to have problems with it.

This is the discovery that Ozzy and Sharon Osbourne made when the decision was undertaken to remove the original tracks by bassist Bob Daisley and drummer Lee Kerslake from *Blizzard of Ozz* and *Diary of a Madman*. The albums were reissued in 2002 with the original bass and drums taken away and new ones recorded over them by bassist Robert Trujillo and drummer Mike Bordin. Why would they do such a thing? Why would they take two undisputed classic albums and mess around with them? Why? WHY?

According to *Pop Matters*, it all came down to a 1986 legal dispute between Ozzy's camp and the original rhythm section. Daisley and Kerslake said they had never been given songwriting royalties or proper performance credits. For example, the *Diary of a Madman* album's credits say that Rudy Sarzo played the bass and Tommy Aldridge played the drums, even though neither one of them actually played on the album.

Daisley and Kerslake wanted their due. Rather than write the pair a check and watch them go on their merry way, the plan was undertaken to replace their performances on both albums. Sharon Osbourne released a statement explaining why this was.

"Because of [Daisley and Kerslake's] abusive and unjust behavior, Ozzy wanted to remove them from these recordings," the statement said. "We turned a negative into a positive by adding a fresh sound to the original albums."

Few were impressed, and for many longtime fans, this was an act of heresy

akin to taking Michelangelo's *David* and replacing his plaster manhood with a Jeff Stryker model dildo. Writing in *Pop Matters*, journalist Adrien Begrand did not mince words when describing the situation.

"Ozzy Osbourne and his manager/wife Sharon have perpetrated one of the most heinous frauds on the record-buying public I have ever witnessed," he wrote. "*Blizzard of Ozz* sounds like a failed experiment. *Diary of a Madman*, on the other hand, is a complete catastrophe . . . *Blizzard of Ozz* and *Diary of a Madman* have been raped of their soul, all just to spite some people they don't like. How classy . . . *Do not buy these albums*."

In his memoir, Ozzy said that the switcheroo was Sharon's idea, and he had nothing to do with the decision. In 2010, he told *Classic Rock* that he had been against the idea and insisted that the original versions of the albums return to store shelves, which they did that year.

How did the guys who re-recorded the tracks feel about it? In 2015, drummer Mike Bordin said that while he didn't want to name any names or get too specific, he was pretty clear in his feelings about the whole kerfuffle.

"I will say this: to hear the original guitar, bass and drum tracks in my headphones while I was recording, was one of the most insane things that I will probably ever experience," he said. "There's a reason why those albums are so good, and why people love them so much. They're magical. That's down to all the guys who made those albums. Far be it from me to ever want to fuck with that. It's something to be treasured."

Mr. Osbourne performs at Ozzfest in 2002. Is he leading the crowd in a group sing-along of the Village People's "YMCA"?

53

"MOM LOVES YOUR STUFF"

THE PRINCE MEETS THE PREZ

MAY 4, 2002

Musicians have visited the White House to hobnob with presidents for many years. Elvis Presley met Richard Nixon in 1970 after writing to him that he had "done an in-depth study of drug abuse and Communist brainwashing techniques," and a decade later, Willie Nelson went there to meet Jimmy Carter. According to the *Los Angeles Times*, he smoked a joint on the White House roof with the president's son Chip, and the former president described said joint as "a big fat Austin torpedo."

The weirdest pairing was almost certainly Ozzy Osbourne and former U.S. President

George W. Bush. Osbourne was there in 2002 at the invitation of Fox News to attend the White House Correspondents' Association dinner, and according to the *Daily News*, he "shuffled and mumbled his way through the evening."

Much jocularity was lobbed back and forth between the vocalist and the forty-third president of the United States. Sharon Osbourne told the *Daily News* that her husband had advised the head of state to grow his hair long. The president retorted that he might do so for his second term. But the biggest laughs of the evening came when the former president addressed the crowd to talk about the evening's special guest.

"The thing about Ozzy is, he's made a lot of big hit recordings," Bush said. "'Party With the Animals,' 'Sabbath Bloody Sabbath,' 'Facing Hell,' 'Black Skies' and 'Bloodbath in Paradise.' Ozzy, Mom loves your stuff." The former president also commented on a photo of himself posing with a woman in a burqa, joking that it was "me and Hillary Clinton."

While Osbourne is the frequent subject of jokes about his memory, his son Jack told Fox News in 2020 that the dinner was one of the highlights of his father's life and that he was still proud of it almost two decades later.

"He still talks about it often," Jack said. "I think it was a pretty big deal for him. My dad and how he was growing up, it was very blue-collar, very working-class. . . . I think the fact that you're all of a sudden being invited to the White House Correspondents' Dinner and President Bush is up there giving you a call out, that was kind of cool. . . . My dad was just blown away by it. It was a very proud moment for him."

Jack Osbourne went on to say that the moment was the culmination of a long journey that his father had embarked upon decades before. Like his former Black Sabbath bandmates, the singer had grown up in abject poverty, and without music, he would have had very

little to lift him out of his circumstances and improve his life.

"He's had a really remarkable story from growing up in a tiny, two-bedroom house with eight people living in it to having a 50-year career and meeting the president of the United States," he told Fox News. "Whether you like his music or not, it's still an amazing story of success."

Ozzy at the 2002 White House Correspondents, Dinner, where he received some good-natured razzing by George W. Bush.

54

SHARON GETS CANCER

. . . AND HANDLES THE NEWS WITH APLOMB

JULY 3, 2002

In July 2002, the newly ascendant Osbourne family was rocked by some terrifying news. Sharon, the family matriarch, had been diagnosed with colon cancer.

In many families, a cancer diagnosis causes the afflicted person and the caregiver to retreat into quiet privacy while they try to slay the tumorous beast. But the Osbourne family is not like other families, and rather than insist on privacy, Sharon told *People* magazine that the entire ordeal would be filmed and made part of *The Osbournes*.

When she revealed her diagnosis, she did her best to make light of it.

"Why'd they have to find it in my bum, of all places?" she asked *People* magazine. "It's embarrassing. I mean, why couldn't I have had a cute heart-shaped polyp on my vagina?"

Why indeed. In any case, while she handled the news with commendable aplomb, her husband did not. He may have been the Prince of Darkness, but his wife was the woman who had saved him from drinking himself to death after his firing from Black Sabbath and given him a career and three children. According to Sharon, he did not take the news well.

"He was hysterical, just terrified," she said. "The doctor had to come over and sedate him."

When she spoke with *People*, she had already undergone surgery on July 3, 2002, to remove a section of her colon measuring a foot in length. Less than a week later, she was informed that doctors had discovered during the surgery that the cancer had spread, and she would need to undergo months of chemotherapy.

Ozzy said he wanted to stay by her side during the ordeal and postponed the first two dates on that year's Ozzfest to

be with her. She would have none of it, and she told her husband to go out there and do the tour, which he did.

Like her husband, Sharon is herself a recovering alcoholic, and in her *People* interview, she described herself as a "*connoisseur*" of fatty junk food. Her doctors said that these two factors combined had increased her cancer risk, but she had no time for couldas, wouldas, or shouldas.

"I can't regret whatever's in the past," she said, resolving to beat the illness and forge ahead. "I have a million more things I'm going to do. And I'm not going anywhere."

Ultimately, she was right. She didn't go anywhere, and she proceeded to do a million more things. That was good for Ozzy, who said plainly that he wouldn't know what to do if she were to pass away before him.

"I've always had a plan that I'd get sick before she did, that I'd die before she did," he said. "But my plan didn't work out. She's my soulmate. If anything did happen to her first, I wouldn't get married again. Sharon and Ozzy, we're a team."

Finally, he summed up the situation in the inimitable way that only Ozzy Osbourne could.

"Life has a way of kicking you in the nuts," he said.

PLUS:

JULY 29, 2002

People

EXCLUSIVE

Sharon Osbourne's CANCER BATTLE

The star of TV's hottest show talks frankly about colon cancer, chemo and her family's love. Says Ozzy: 'She's my whole world'

ARE THEY OR AREN'T THEY? J.Lo & Ben and other couples who keep fans guessing

PARTY IN PARIS Gwyneth and pals at the fashion shows

BOOK EXCERPT

THE FINAL MOMENTS OF 9/11's FLIGHT 93

Sharon in 2008 at the Stand Up to Cancer Gala in Hollywood. She had been diagnosed with the disease herself and kicked its tumorous ass to the curb.

141

55

OVER-PRESCRIBE THE MOUNTAIN

OZZY AND THE OVER-ZEALOUS PRESCRIBER

DECEMBER 7, 2003

Ozzy and Sharon at Chicago's Wrigley Field in 2003, where Ozzy sang "Take Me Out to the Ball Game." SPOILER ALERT: It was bad.

In the summer of 2003, Ozzy Osbourne appeared at a baseball game at Chicago's Wrigley Field. He had been invited to sing "Take Me Out to the Ball Game" during the seventh-inning stretch, and the kindest phrase you could use to describe his performance would be to say that he gruesomely murdered it.

The culprit, it turned out, was prescription drugs. Or rather, dozens of prescription drugs.

The many, many pills had been prescribed by one Dr. David A. Kipper of Beverly Hills, and they caused the singer to be in what the Los Angeles Times called "a perpetual stupor." It was in that state that television audiences saw him on the hit show The Osbournes.

Many viewers chalked up his incoherent, mumbling state to the residual effects of being a rock star for four decades. The truth was that it was Valium, Dexedrine, Mysoline, Adderall, and many more very heavy-duty prescription medications, in a daily regimen that the singer estimated had him taking over forty pills a day at its height.

"I was wiped out on pills," he said. "I couldn't talk. I couldn't walk. I could barely stand up. I was lumbering about like the Hunchback of Notre Dame."

The irony was that Osbourne had initially sought out Kipper to help him get off prescription drugs. The doctor put the singer on a ten-day detox course, and the relationship might well have ended right there. But when Sharon Osbourne was diagnosed with cancer, Ozzy fell prey to anxiety and depression, and the number of medicines Kipper prescribed to the singer skyrocketed.

The singer said that he fired the doctor in September 2003 after over a year of regularly being on the receiving end of his extreme quackery. The California state medical board revoked Kipper's medical license three months later, accusing him of gross negligence. But boy howdy did he get while the getting was good. The doctor made $650,000 off Osbourne for services rendered, plus another $58,000 for the medications.

Sharon Osbourne said that she decided to terminate Kipper's services after the incident at Wrigley Field. However, the situation had been unacceptable for a long time before then.

"Ozzy was overmedicated," she said. "He couldn't speak. He couldn't walk. He was falling over. Ozzy would call Kipper and tell him how bad he was feeling, and Kipper would say: 'Take five more of those and 10 more of these.' It was insane."

Ozzy ended up seeking out the services of Dr. Allan Ropper, who was then chief of neurology at Caritas St. Elizabeth's Medical Center in Boston. Osbourne described Ropper as "flabbergasted" at the number of pills he had been prescribed. Ropper was eventually able to get Ozzy off all of the medications Kipper had prescribed.

"Looking back on it now, I see Dr. Kipper as sort of a friendly villain," the singer said. "He comes off as a really nice guy—that is, until you get the bill."

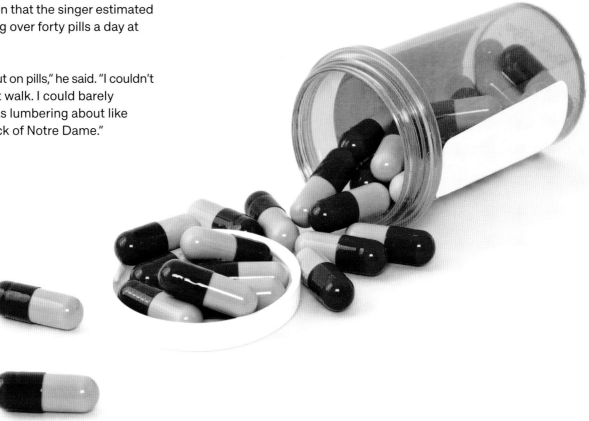

56

THE QUAD BIKE ACCIDENT

GOING OFF THE RAILS IN AN ATV

DECEMBER 8, 2003

By 2003, it was probably accurate to say that Ozzy Osbourne had cheated death a kajillion times. However, in December of that year, it looked like his luck might have finally run out. Under the headline "Rock'n'roll Ozzy hurt in quad-bike accident," the *Guardian* reported that the singer had been injured in an ATV mishap outside his Buckinghamshire home and sustained a broken neck vertebra.

A publicist speaking on Osbourne's behalf, Cindy Guagenti, said that the injuries were even more extensive. She said that his collarbone and multiple ribs were broken, and at the hospital, he underwent some procedures that revealed how extensively he had been injured.

"Osbourne was at Wexham Park hospital in Slough last night having an operation to lift his collarbone, which was believed to be resting on a major artery and interrupting blood flow to his arm," the *Guardian*'s Mark Oliver wrote. "Surgeons were also trying to stem bleeding into his lungs."

The injuries were not considered life-threatening, but he would pay for them in other ways for the rest of his life. As you will learn as you make your way through the pages of the weighty volume you now hold in your hands, the injury would account for complications and chronic pain that he would suffer for years to come.

At the time, few people were thinking about how the accident would affect Osbourne in the coming years, and not just because that was difficult to foresee. The terrible, terrible problem that many people were fixated on was that season three of *The Osbournes* was in production at the time of the accident, and his recovery might interfere with filming.

The accident also took place on the day that the singer's duet with his daughter Kelly was released as a single. It was a cover of Black Sabbath's "Changes," and if the singer had not survived the accident, it could have taken on an unintended macabre overtone. Osbourne's account of the accident in his memoir made it clear that death was a very strong possibility, and the fact that he survived the accident was almost certainly a matter of pure luck.

"The front wheels hit a pothole, my right hand slipped off the handlebar and slammed into the lever, the engine went fucking crazy, and the whole thing shot out from under me and did a backflip in the air, throwing me on to the grass," he wrote. "For about a millionth of a second, I thought, Oh well, that wasn't so bad. . . . Then the bike landed on top of me."

Interestingly, Osbourne said that responsibility for the accident lay with one man—Adolf Hitler. He said that the pothole that had caused the accident resulted from a bomb that had been dropped during World War II, and the area was full of them. Apparently, pilots for the Thousand Year Reich were enormous cowards. Rather than go on bombing raids over highly populated and protected cities, they would sometimes drop their bombs over sparsely populated areas where no one would shoot at them. Ozzy's house, unfortunately, was built in such an area.

Ozzy wrote that the doctors had to put him into a "chemical coma" for over a week because the pain would have been unbearable. He remarked upon that with his trademark wry humor.

"If I'd copped it then, it would have been a fitting end for me," he said. "I'd spent my whole adult life trying to get into a chemical coma."

If he can't keep four wheels right side down, how wise are two? Ozzy clowns on a chopper in December of 2003, the same month as his quad accident.

57

PRINCE OF DARKNESS

A CAREER RETROSPECTIVE FEATURING MISS PIGGY

MARCH 22, 2005

In 2005, Ozzy Osbourne rang in thirty-five years without working in a slaughterhouse with *Prince of Darkness*, a four-disc retrospective box set that provides an overview of his entire career up to that point. It was an opportunity to document the music of one of rock 'n' roll's true legends, and with so many more fans on board after *The Osbournes*, he had never had a bigger audience. But would this box set be designed with longtime fans in mind or people who had just jumped on the bandwagon because of *The Osbournes*?

The answer is—the latter. It's clear from a cursory glance at the tracklist that the decision to undertake this compilation was meant to capitalize on Osbourne's status as a dysfunctional TV dad.

This is not to say that the music on this box isn't any good or that there are no surprises. The first two discs of *Prince of Darkness* cover mostly well-worn ground, although those beyond casual fans will be interested to hear the demos and live material. The live stuff, in particular, is worth checking out.

Those who have heard the *Tribute* album are already familiar with the live cuts on disc one, such as "I Don't Know" and "Flying High Again," but any opportunity to hear Randy Rhoads in a live setting is a good one. The live material on disc two comes from *The Ultimate Ozzy*, a "video album" released in the VHS era that was recorded in Kansas City on April 1, 1986. Ozzy famously never liked *The Ultimate Sin*, so one assumes these are his preferred versions of some of these songs.

The quality of the set takes an abrupt and precipitous nosedive on disc three. It compiles various recordings featuring Osbourne and various special guests, and it's titled "With Friends," which is inaccurate because if you're the Prince of Darkness, you should have no friends, just victims being tormented in your dungeon.

A couple of these collaborations, such as his version of Status Quo's "Pictures of Matchstick Men," which he recorded with Type O Negative, are interesting and could conceivably get listened to repeatedly. Unfortunately, songs like

Ozzy and the symbolic blue brick used in the video for a 2005 charity recording of "Tears in Heaven." Since Sharon organized the benefit, it must have been hard to say no.

that are hopelessly outnumbered by things like "Born to Be Wild," which comes from the *Kermit Unplugged* album and features vocal contributions from Miss Piggy. It shares disc three with a cover of the Bee Gees' "Stayin' Alive" and "Dog, The Bounty Hunter," which mercifully lasts less than a minute.

The fourth and final disc is called "Under Cover," and it consists of—you guessed it—covers of other people's songs. The songs that fare the best are the headbangers, like King Crimson's "21st Century Schizoid Man" and Mountain's "Mississippi Queen." Ozzy's voice and approach fit comfortably within these songs, something it doesn't do when he tries his hand at the Beatles' "In My Life," Buffalo Springfield's "For What It's Worth," or John Lennon's "Working Class Hero."

The disc ends the set with Black Sabbath's "Changes," which features daughter Kelly Osbourne. Some of the lyrics were changed for this version, so Sabbath purists will have multiple reasons to take umbrage with the recording. Kelly sings, "I love you daddy, but I've found my way," perhaps referring to her 2002 album *Shut Up* and the solo career that it was intended to inspire. As tempting as it may be to slam the entire effort to turn Kelly Osbourne into a solo act, she does just fine on the song—nothing revolutionary, but certainly not the horrifying crime against humanity that critics made it out to be.

Prince of Darkness is not a bad way for the uninitiated to get to know Ozzy's solo output, provided they stick to the first two discs. The less said about the third

disc, the better. As for "Under Cover," it was released as a standalone disc with four more tracks added, such as "Rocky Mountain Way" by Joe Walsh and "Sunshine of Your Love" by Cream. The added tracks are mediocre and don't add value to the disc, but they increase the running time, so you're getting "more" with that version.

Long story short, *Prince of Darkness* should be considered a solid two-disc set that comes with two other discs that you are highly unlikely to listen to twice.

58

IT'S NOT A BAT HEAD EITHER

I CAN'T BELIEVE IT'S NOT BUTTER! GETS A NEW SPOKESMAN

FEBRUARY 20, 2006

Getting famous from being on *The Osbournes* gave Ozzy a level of access to the mainstream that he had never had before. Yes, he had been a million-selling rock star for decades, but when he became the star of the TV show, people who had never listened to a note of his music began welcoming him and his family into their homes every week. In fact, the success was so far-reaching that even people who didn't know he was a musician suddenly knew him by name.

Among those who tried to cash in on this situation was Upfield Holdings BV, better known as Unilever Foods, the people who gave us I Can't Believe It's Not Butter! While they had been using literary figure Fabio as their celebrity spokesman since 1994, his flowing locks, shirtless chest, and chiseled physique had been in their employ for more than a decade, and maybe it was time to shake things up. Ozzy was thus drafted for a television commercial.

The ad featured the singer and an Ozzy Osbourne impersonator named Jon Culshaw in a kitchen, baking pastries. The impersonator goes to the refrigerator to fetch them both butter and is confronted with the choice between the genuine article and the butter substitute, which is in a new psychedelic container. He chooses the fake stuff after first saying he can't tell the difference, and together they make a concoction called "Fairy Cakes."

The product was being relaunched at the time with a new recipe and new packaging. The commercial spot was intended to inform consumers of this fact, and according to *Blabbermouth*, the company spent seven million British pounds on the ad campaign. Brand manager Noam Buchalter explained the meaning of the commercial in case someone somewhere was unable to follow the trail of clues.

"'I Can't Believe It's Not Butter' now tastes so much like butter that the two Ozzies can't tell the difference," he said. "'I Can't Believe It's Not Butter' has always been a great impersonator of butter and proud of it. Who better to star in the ads than the UK's best impersonator? Jon and Ozzy make a great double act and their infectious personalities will have a great impact on consumers."

While *Consumer Reports* never tackled the thorny question of whether or not

The good people who make I Can't Believe It's Not Butter! somehow roped Ozzy into making a commercial on the occasion of their groovy new packaging.

Ozzy's appearance in the commercial helped sell more I Can't Believe It's Not Butter!, it may have had one unintended side effect. In 2008, two years after the Ozzy commercial first aired, John Lydon, better known as Johnny Rotten from the Sex Pistols, appeared in a television commercial for Country Life butter.

Sadly, if the events were related, the trend stopped right there. No further shock rockers, punk rockers, or other rockers became brand ambassadors for either butter or I Can't Believe It's Not Butter! Perhaps that's best since Wendy O. Williams, G.G. Allin, and El Duce are not around to make them.

Donny and Marie Osmond join Ozzy to shill for Pepsi during a 2003 Super Bowl commercial. The Tampa Bay Buccaneers won.

59

RESPECT

BLACK SABBATH MAKES THE ROCK AND ROLL HALL OF FAME

MARCH 13, 2006

On March 13, 2006, the four original members of Black Sabbath got something that had eluded them for decades. No, it wasn't the opportunity for them all to be on the same stage simultaneously, although that happened as part of it. No, it was the respect of the chattering classes, which they finally won in the form of their induction into the Rock and Roll Hall of Fame.

The band had been eligible for induction on more than one occasion but never garnered enough votes. The situation was so absurd that in 1999, Ozzy wrote to the Rock and Roll Hall of Fame and told them not to bother with the band at all.

"Just take our name off the list," he wrote. "Save the ink. Forget about us."

The singer characterized the nomination as "meaningless" because regular music fans had nothing to do with who got nominated or inducted. It was industry types and the media, both of whom he said "never bought an album or concert ticket in their lives." Considering that the band had been critically savaged yet beloved by fans for its entire career, he had a point.

"Black Sabbath has never been media darlings," he said. "We're a people's band and that suits us just fine."

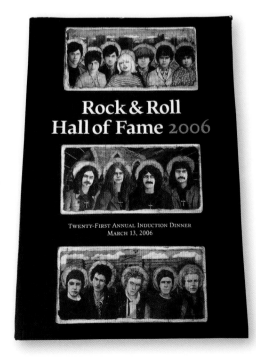

Seven years later, the band got inducted, and Ozzy was on board with it. He told *Rolling Stone* that it had been a mistake for him to speak unilaterally on behalf of the other guys.

"We'd get nominated, but never get in," he said. "So it's like you're in a race and you're nearly at the finishing line and someone comes up and kicks you in the nuts before you cross it.... But I realized I don't have the right to speak for Black Sabbath. All I am is the singer . . . I didn't have the right to say that, and I truly apologize."

The band was inducted by James Hetfield and Lars Ulrich of Metallica when the night came. In his speech, a clearly excited Ulrich said something that was true of countless bands that had formed in the previous thirty-five years.

"Bill, Geezer, Ozzy, and Tony, if it weren't for you, we wouldn't be here," he said. "Obviously, if there was no Black Sabbath, there would be no Metallica, and if there was no Black Sabbath, hard rock and heavy metal as we know it today would look, sound, and be shaped very, very differently. . . . Black Sabbath is and always will be synonymous with the term 'heavy metal.'"

The band members kept their comments brief as they accepted the award, and during the television broadcast, the cameras flashed to Osbourne's family numerous times. If they didn't all look 100 percent attentive about this momentous occasion, that would have fit in well with the singer's feelings about parental accomplishments in general.

"I think they're happy," he said. "I've had platinum discs, I've had Grammys, so I suppose they're kind of spoiled to the fact that daddy goes out one day and he comes back with another award. I'm not saying that to be bigheaded; it's just that they're all into their own thing. When I was their age, if my dad did anything, I didn't want to fucking know."

The original lineup of Black Sabbath gets inducted into the Rock and Roll Hall of Fame in 2006. It was about time too.

60

BLACK RAIN

OZZY RECORDS
WHILE SOBER

MAY 22, 2007

Ozzy raises the roof at Holland's Fields of Rock festival in 2007.

2007's *Black Rain* marked some significant changes in Ozzy Osbourne's life. For one thing, he had been doing Ozzfest for several years now, and in the period of 2000–2006, he shared stages with some of metal's hardest hitters, including Slipknot, Pantera, and System of a Down. The abrasive, mechanical sounds of those bands had definitely had an effect, and from the first song on the album, "Not Going Away," it was clear that those bands had rubbed off on him somewhat.

The other significant change was that it was the first album he had ever recorded while sober. So what's the verdict? Did the lack of drugs and alcohol make him dig deep and focus on producing the greatest album of his career? Or was he completely unable to function in the studio without drugs and alcohol, a possibility that might be revealed if he came up with a lousy album?

The answer is somewhere in the middle. As far as Ozzy's vocal performance goes, he's as strong as ever, and there are moments at which he seems more focused and in control than he had been in a long time. The problem is that what surrounds him on this album is not always great. It seems at times to be a little derivative of Marilyn Manson, in the sense that it's down-tuned metal with random electronic noises, and it's hard to escape the conclusion that it's a sop to being "current." Luckily, Ozzy's voice is so distinctive that it's unlikely anyone hearing this album thought it was made by someone else.

Production complaints aside, there's some very good stuff on *Black Rain*. The album fares best on songs like "I Don't Wanna Stop" and "11 Silver," which are pretty straightforward and energetic rockers, but it suffers when the kitchen sink gets thrown into the proceedings, as happens on "The Almighty Dollar."

The issue, it seems, is not that this was Ozzy's first album recorded while sober. No, the issue is that it was his first album recorded in his home studio with ProTools. There are a lot of extraneous noises and sounds mucking up the proceedings, and if you've ever seen anyone tinker long into the night with a new musical gadget, then you may agree that was the dynamic at play here.

Critics generally didn't care for the album. Andy Greene of *Rolling Stone* gave it two and a half stars and hoped there would just be a Black Sabbath reunion at some point soon. *Sputnikmusic* gave it one and a half stars in a review that sounded like an oncologist recommending that Osbourne be put into hospice care. The reviews were pretty brutal across the

board, but the fact remains that *Black Rain* is a decent and entertaining album that never drags in its forty-six minutes.

Despite the slings and arrows of the critics, *Black Rain* was the highest-debuting album of Ozzy's career to that point, and "I Don't Wanna Stop" became the official theme song of World Wrestling Entertainment's 2007 "Judgment Day" event. It also appeared on the soundtrack to the *Madden NFL 08* video game and on the *Guitar Hero* video game. So in typical fashion, it was only the critics that didn't like it, and you were not about to see the newly sober Ozzy cry into his near-beer over that.

PART 6

WRITIN', REUNIONS', AND RETIREMENTS, 2010–2019

Ozzy comes to the land of the ice and snow (also known as Norway) in 2012 to perform at the Bergenhus Festning. "Festning" is Norwegian for "fortress." You're welcome.

61

I AM OZZY

THE BRUMMIE PENS A MEMOIR

JANUARY 25, 2010

It was forty years after the release of the debut Black Sabbath album and thirty years after the release of *Blizzard of Ozz*. Ozzy Osbourne had conquered the world and truly made it his bitch, but one problem remained. There were a lot of rumors and innuendo out there about things the singer had done, things he hadn't done, and things that might have had some partial truth to them.

Osbourne himself sets the record straight in his 2010 memoir, *I Am Ozzy*. Its eleven chapters describe everything from his impoverished upbringing to his days conquering the world with Black Sabbath to the triumphs of his solo career. It also describes the many scandalous details of his life, some of which are confirmed in its pages for the first time anywhere.

Written in the same style in which Osbourne speaks, the book is a warts-and-all account of his life. It makes no attempt whatsoever to sanitize any of the events of his life or glamorize them. For example, when he recounts getting thrown out of Dachau concentration camp for his drunken behavior—yes, that actually happened—he acknowledges that there was no excuse for it and that his conduct had been uniquely unacceptable.

"I must be the only person in history who's ever been thrown out of that fucking place," he guessed, and one assumes that he was probably right.

I Am Ozzy also offers the first opportunity for general readers to get into details about the plane crash that killed Randy Rhoads. While eyewitness accounts from people like Don Airey have been out there for years, this is the first opportunity readers have had to get Ozzy's complete take in depth. It also offers a closer view of how much the incident was a "before" and "after" moment in his life. His career went on, and he went from triumph to triumph, but on a personal level, it's clear that he never really recovered from that day in March 1982. He dedicates the book to the fans first and foremost, but the dedication to his former guitar player still stings to read.

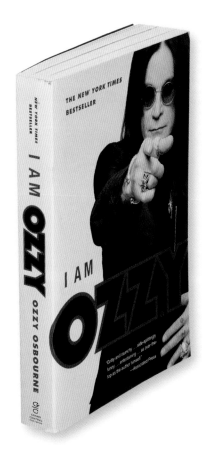

"And not forgetting the one special guy who meant so much to me, Mr. Randy Rhoads, R.I.P.," he wrote. "I will never forget you and I hope we meet again somewhere, somehow."

I Am Ozzy is a quick and absorbing read, and everyone from diehard to casual fans should enjoy it. On the next excursion to your local neighborhood bookstore, do yourself a solid and thumb through a few pages. It's never boring, it's written with sincere humility, and it shows that for all the ups, downs, and unforced errors, he's been a pretty lucky guy.

Seriously, read the book. His story is about ten million times crazier than you think.

Esteemed literary figure Ozzy Osbourne launches his memoir, *I Am Ozzy*, in London.

62

SCREAM

AT LEAST THEY DIDN'T CALL IT *SOUL SUCKA*

JUNE 11, 2010

Ozzy at Dodger Stadium in 2010 leading the fans in a "Scream for a Cure" to raise awareness for cancer research. It was wicked loud.

Ozzy Osbourne's first album of the 2010s, *Scream* faced some opposition from fans before it even came out. In the run-up to its release, word got out that it would be called *Soul Sucka*, and Ozzy's fans staged a mild revolt.

"When we put that on the Internet none of my fan base liked the title," Osbourne told *Rolling Stone*. "They were like, 'I can't imagine me walking around the fucking house with the words 'Soul Sucka' on my T-shirt.' So I was like, 'Fuck it. I've got to come up with something else!'"

If the only problem with the album had been the title, then this story would have a happy ending. Sadly, the very stupid original title is probably the least objectionable thing about *Scream*. It's not a disaster of an album, it just sounds like a lot of songwriting and production choices were made to keep Ozzy "current." Those choices were bizarre at the time, and they have not aged very well.

Part of the issue may be that Osbourne is working with a completely different group of musicians this time out. Unlike

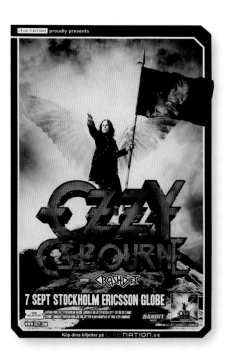

previous lineups—notably Wylde-Trujillo-Bordin—it doesn't really sound like a band. It sounds like a bunch of different sidemen who all came in to play with ProTools.

It's a shame because the individual musicians do a good job here. Guitarist Gus G. is a more than capable replacement for the recently departed Zakk Wylde, and he produces nasty riff after nasty riff. He can play. However, it all sounds kind of tacked on after the fact, and it loses a lot of its bite when it gets wholly drowned in sound effects, as it does in "Crucify."

The majority of *Scream* sadly fares the same way, and it's frustrating. It feels like a lot of effort was put into the production and songwriting, but it just doesn't work for whatever reason. All of the elements are there, but the end result feels like a bunch of ingredients instead of a fully cooked meal.

The album closes with "I Love You All," which actually has an interesting melody and looks like it might go in some interesting direction and possibly redeem the album . . . and then it's over

after barely a minute. So the food is terrible, and such small portions.

While the album may have missed the mark when it came to the music, the promotional efforts were totally on point. Three songs, "Let Me Hear You Scream," "Soul Sucker," and "Diggin' Me Down," were made available for the *Rock Band* video game, and the day of the album's release, Osbourne turned up at a baseball game at Dodger Stadium, where he asked the throngs in attendance to scream the album title as forcefully as possible, for as long as possible.

The continuous scream was measured by Stuart Claxton of Guinness World Records, who declared it the longest on record at approximately two minutes. The singer was then awarded a certificate that read, "The Guinness World Record led by Ozzy Osbourne for the longest scream by a crowd was broken at Dodger Stadium in Los Angeles, California, USA on June 11, 2010."

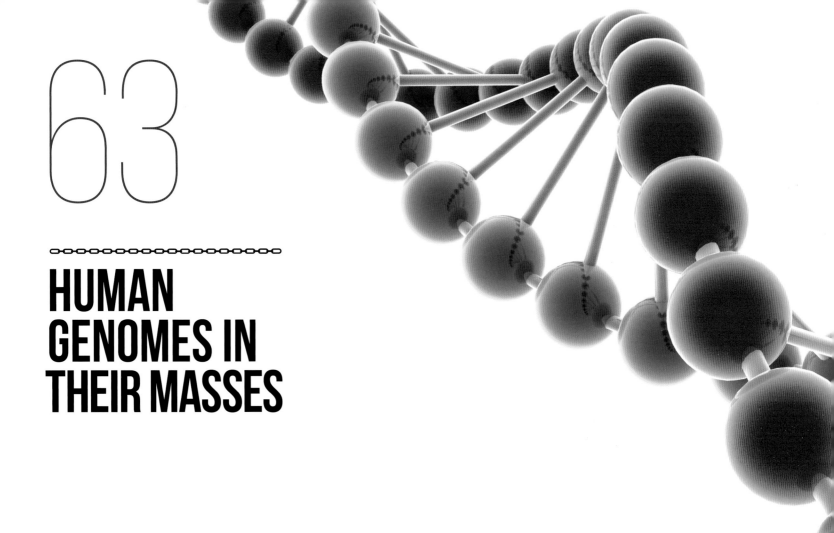

63

HUMAN GENOMES IN THEIR MASSES

SCIENCE TRIES TO FIND OUT WHY OZZY'S NOT DEAD YET

JUNE 15, 2010

Since the beginning of time, many questions have plagued the human race. Is there a god? What omen will foretell the apocalypse? And perhaps most of all, how is Ozzy Osbourne still alive?

Osbourne is in the same category as Jimmy Page, Keith Richards, and Alice Cooper, all of whom ingested ungodly amounts of drugs and alcohol and are still here today to talk about it. Very few people who were similarly enthusiastic about controlled substances lived to see their twenty-eighth birthday, yet these musicians are still alive and kicking. But why?

In 2010, scientists looked for the answer by performing a full genome analysis on Osbourne's DNA. The goal was to figure out how he had managed not to die, despite living "a lifestyle that would likely kill any other human being," per

Rolling Stone. The test, conducted by the Massachusetts genome researchers Knome, used a sample of his blood to shed light on how his body reacted to harmful chemicals.

In the *Sunday Times of London*, Osbourne himself said that he was curious about the results of the analysis and what they might turn up.

"I was curious," he said. "Given the swimming pools of booze I've guzzled over the years—not to mention all of the cocaine, morphine, sleeping pills, cough syrup, LSD, Rohypnol . . . you name it— there's really no plausible medical reason why I should still be alive."

According to geneticist Nathaniel Pearson, Osbourne has several unique gene variants. Some affect how the Prince of Darkness responds to drugs and alcohol. Genes connected to addiction, alcoholism, and absorption of marijuana, opiates, and methamphetamines also had unique variations.

"He had a change on the regulatory region of the ADH4 gene, a gene associated with alcoholism, that we've never seen before," Knome co-founder Jorge Conde told *ABC News*. "He has an increased predisposition for alcohol dependence of something like six times higher. He also had a slight increased risk for cocaine addiction, but he dismissed that. He said that if anyone has done as much cocaine as he had, they would have been hooked."

The scientists also found that the singer has Neanderthal genes. This is not

to say "Neanderthal" in the sense of "ME SAVAGE HEAVY METAL CAVEMAN WHO BITE HEAD OFF DOVE!" It's "Neanderthal" in the sense of *Homo sapiens neanderthalensis*, the subspecies of humans who went extinct forty thousand years ago.

"In east Asia and Europe, a lot of us have a little Neanderthal ancestry," said geneticist Nathaniel Pearson, who worked on the study. "We found a sliver of the genes in Ozzy."

Despite his ability to effortlessly metabolize amounts of drugs and alcohol that could kill a baby elephant, the study found that he did have one Achilles' heel—he's a slow metabolizer of

caffeine. So while he can ingest *Scarface*-sized snowdrifts of cocaine to no ill effect, one cup of coffee will ruin his entire day. So if he drops by your house for some reason, offer him a juice box or a bottle of Poland Spring rather than a steaming mug of the fair-trade stuff. You don't want a jittery Ozzy on your hands.

Achtung! Ozzy at a 2010 autograph session in Berlin to promote his album *Scream*. Looks like the edibles just kicked in too.

64

SEE OZZY AND SHARON'S HOME, WHICH YOU WILL NEVER AFFORD

THE OSBOURNES GET INTO REAL ESTATE PORN

JUNE 1, 2011

Ozzy's former home in Beverly Hills, which was purchased in 2007 by Christina Aguilera. Rather than preserve the heavy metal décor, she painted the house pink immediately upon moving in.

The Osbournes' Buckinghamshire home, which was burglarized in 2004. While some might play it safe and avoid engaging a burglar, Ozzy actually got the guy in a headlock! Don't fuck with Ozzy, people. He's been to jail.

In June 2011, Ozzy and Sharon Osbourne had an honor bestowed upon them that has eluded most people who have at one point in their lives been described as "shock rockers." Their sprawling Los Angeles home was featured in the august pages of *Architectural Digest*, a publication not known for featuring the likes of Blackie Lawless or Oderus Urungus.

The publication clarified that the home featured in its June 2011 issue was not the one fans of *The Osbournes* were used to seeing every week. That home, whose decor the article described as "Contemporary Goth," became so well known to fans that interior designer Martyn Lawrence-Bullard said the famous couple needed to find somewhere more remote to live.

"They would have carloads of fans driving by at three in the morning screaming, 'Ozzy, we love you!' outside the front door," he said. By 2011, the couple had become empty-nesters, with their children Jack and Kelly all grown up and in homes and careers of their own. It made sense for Ozzy and Sharon to seek out new digs with more quiet and privacy, and for that, they chose the gated community of Hidden Hills in Los Angeles's San Fernando Valley.

Sharon said that while her new home had stunning views of the Pacific Ocean, the couple needed help decluttering and making a home that felt more welcoming than the previous place. They weren't hoarders, but they had accumulated a ton of random crap over the years, leading Sharon to compare it to "a furniture shop." She asked Lawrence-Bullard to help them pare down and decide what to hang on to or get rid of.

"I said to Martyn, 'Please make my house a home,'" she said. "'Tell me, what do I lose and what do I keep, and where do I put it all?'"

The interior designer designated the living room the home's main attraction, saying it was where the singer liked to paint due to the abundant sunlight that pours into the space in the daytime. If you didn't know he liked to paint, you might also not know that Sharon is a collector of antique dolls and puppets from Italy, and they make their home in the living room as well.

If Ozzy has an "accomplishment area" in the house, it would have to be the staircase located just off the living room, which is surrounded by gold and platinum records that have been hung around it. So if Ozzy's imposter syndrome starts acting up, all he needs to do is walk up and down the stairs, which are surrounded by gleaming, framed mementos of his many career highlights.

The biggest surprise is likely the master bedroom. While many might expect Ozzy to sleep inside a coffin in a rat-infested mausoleum lit with torches, it looks more like where *Baby One More Time*–era Britney Spears would get her eight hours of shut-eye a night.

"Can you believe the Prince of Darkness sleeps in a mirrored four-poster bed, with lilac painted-silk walls and satin curtains?" Lawrence-Bullard said. Luckily, it has at least one attribute that proves it's not a totally Ozzy-free zone—a button at the bedside that causes a massive television to appear in front of him like the monolith in *2001: A Space Odyssey*.

"He loves lying in bed watching the History Channel," the designer explained. "And *Hoarders*."

65

NEVER SAY NEVER!

BLACK SABBATH ACTUALLY, REALLY, HONESTLY REUNITES

NOVEMBER 11, 2011

The day was November 11, 2011. The city was Los Angeles. And at the legendary Whiskey A Go Go, the original lineup of Black Sabbath announced that they would reunite after years and years of false starts. Well, most of them did, anyway.

It's settled law that since the 1984 premiere of the mockumentary *This Is Spinal Tap*, the number "11" is the loudest in the world. For that reason, there was no better day to make the announcement that fans had been waiting for than November 11, 2011, or 11/11/11 if you're writing a check. That announcement was that the original lineup of Black Sabbath was really and truly going to reunite, tour, and make a new album.

The band had made a couple of attempts at a reunion before. In 1985, they performed at Live Aid, and in 1997, they recorded two live dates and two studio tracks that ended up on the 1998 *Reunion* album. Both times, anyone hoping for a full tour or a new studio album was disappointed, but they could always console themselves with the fact that maybe next time, it would all work out. Well, by 2011, all of the band members were getting on in years, and the sense that there would be no "next time" was hard to escape. It was now or never.

The four original members gave a press conference to tell the drooling fans why they had decided to reunite and what to expect. On the first score, Ozzy simply said that the time was right, and on the second, bassist Geezer Butler said, "It really is back to the old Sabbath style and sound." Awesome sauce.

Or not. In early 2012, Sabbath mainstay guitarist Tony Iommi was diagnosed with lymphoma. Then, a month later, original drummer Bill Ward posted an announcement to his website, saying that he would not participate in the reunion until a piece of paper was put in front of him that was more to his liking.

"I am unable to continue unless a 'signable' contract is drawn up; a contract that reflects some dignity and respect toward me as an original member of the band," he wrote. "I want a contract that shows some respect to me and my family, a

contract that will honor all that I've brought to Black Sabbath since its beginning."

Despite the promise that all four original members would reunite, the band chose to carry on minus Ward, drafting Brad Wilk of Rage Against the Machine to play the drums and choosing Rick Rubin to produce the new album. The drummer for Ozzy's solo band, Tommy Clufetos, was chosen to pound the skins for touring purposes.

For many diehards, this meant it was not a proper reunion, it wasn't *really* Sabbath, and they would not attend the concerts, nor would they buy whatever new album was recorded. For everyone else, a replaced drummer was a small indignity to suffer to see 75 percent of the original

lineup, particularly with Iommi suffering from lymphoma and possibly not a lot of time left on this earth.

Fun Fact: Despite Ward's absence from the proceedings, the live concerts put on by this incarnation of the band were phenomenal in the opinion of this author, who saw them in 2013 at Brooklyn's Barclays Center. This author wasn't expecting much and went to the concert more out of respect than anything else, as one visits a dying relative in hospice care. They blew the doors off the place, and for a bunch of guys in their sixties—one of whom was receiving chemotherapy treatments at the time—they absolutely killed.

BLACK SABBATH—*13*

75 PERCENT OF SABBATH'S ORIGINAL LINEUP DOES ONE LAST LAP

JUNE 10, 2013

The Black Sabbath album *13* had a nearly impossible job to do, and it faced almost impossible odds to do it. The first new studio album from the original lineup—minus drummer Bill Ward, which is a pretty significant asterisk—marked the end of a thirty-five-year absence that had begun in 1978 with *Never Say Die!*

That's a long time to be out of the public eye, and during that time, there had been numerous false starts and attempts to get these guys back into the studio. During that time, the Black Sabbath name had stopped meaning Osbourne-Iommi-Butler-Ward and had instead come to mean "Tony Iommi and a very long, perpetually unstable list of singers, bassists, drummers, and keyboard players." The album was, among many things, an attempt to restore the Black Sabbath name to what it had meant originally, even if Bill Ward didn't take part.

Let's get this part out of the way right now—*13* is not as good as anything in the band's classic 70s catalog, an expectation that may never really have been realistic anyway. If you listen to it back to back with, say, *Master of Reality*, you will still prefer *Master of Reality*.

Having said that, *13* beats the living shit out of *Technical Ecstasy* and is a good album in its own right. Just don't listen to it expecting the next "Iron Man" or the next "Sweet Leaf" or the next "War Pigs." It isn't here. Still, there are good moments on this album, and it's an entertaining listen that rarely bores.

In a 2021 interview with *Spin*, Sabbath guitarist Tony Iommi said that producer Rick Rubin wanted the band to go back to their original raw style, asking if they still had their old amplifiers from fifty years previous and preferring a bare-bones production style.

"He just wanted it very bare and very basic, which you know, was good," Iommi said.

The raw style goes a long way. Hearing Ozzy's voice on top of Iommi's grinding guitar tone is a treat in and of itself, and unlike a lot of Osbourne's solo albums, the production is entirely unobtrusive—the instruments actually sound like instruments. It would have been better if Geezer Butler's bass had been louder in the mix, and no disrespect to Brad Wilk, but he just isn't Bill Ward. But again, these are things that dock the album just a few points—they're not massive flaws that make the record impossible to listen to.

Perhaps in an attempt to recall the band's early days, the standard edition of *13* contains only eight songs at fifty-three minutes, despite it being the compact disc age and most listeners expecting to get seventy-nine minutes of music out of a single disc. The deluxe edition addressed this somewhat with a bonus disc containing another three songs, but it's likely that the idea was to make the proper album recall the turntable days.

So how are the songs themselves? Again, nothing on here stands alongside the band's greatest triumphs, but there's nothing bad either. Openers "End of the Beginning" and "God Is Dead?" would fit perfectly well on any of the original band's albums, and "Zeitgeist" has more than a passing resemblance to *Paranoid*'s "Planet Caravan."

Ozzy with Black Sabbath in Oslo, Norway, in 2013. Sure, they make black metal and burn churches over there, but they could still use a lesson from the pioneers.

The opening riff to "Age of Reason" also gets bonus points for sounding like "Driver 8" by REM, which could not possibly have been intentional. It's a bit of a bummer hearing "Damaged Soul," a waltz-time track that would have swung mightily with Bill Ward pounding the skins, but we can only listen to the competent drumming of Brad Wilk and imagine what might have been. The album wraps up with "Dear Father," which is probably the least remarkable song on the album but for the fact that it ends with thunder and rain sounds, in what one assumes is a tribute to the debut album.

13 is a good effort that might not be up there with *Master of Reality* but is a satisfying listen anyway. It's unlikely to inspire lots and lots and lots of repeat listens, but hey, at least it ended up that the band concluded things as well as they could and didn't leave us with *Forbidden* as the last thing Black Sabbath ever recorded, thank god.

67

CRAZY TRAM

OZZY GETS HIS OWN MASS-TRANSIT CONVEYANCE

MAY 27, 2016

He and his hometown may not have always gotten along, but seeing Ozzy christen his namesake Birmingham tram in 2016 proved that all's well that ends well.

For the first part of Ozzy Osbourne's life, the singer and the town of Birmingham were similarly fond of one another. In other words, the town viewed him as a degenerate and ne'er-do-well, and the singer regarded the town as a great place to abandon. When the two parted company, it would have been tempting to predict them both saying the words "good riddance" simultaneously and in stereo.

Having said that, age, fame, and money will do a lot to make people want to claim you as a favorite son, even people who had once jailed you. That happened for the first time on July 6, 2007, when he became the first person ever to receive a star on the Birmingham Walk

of Stars. It was not his first such star— his first had been on the Hollywood Walk of Fame, which had been awarded to him in 2002—but according to *Birmingham Live*, it was the one he said he cared about more.

"I have a star in Hollywood on their Walk of Fame but having a star in my hometown means so much more to me," he said. Amusingly, the induction ceremony on Birmingham's Broad Street was described on the Walk of Fame's website as taking place in an "Alcohol Restricted Zone."

After Ozzy, the following stars inducted were comedian Jasper Carrott and Noddy Holder of Slade. Ozzy's Black Sabbath bandmate Tony Iommi was inducted the following year, and Geezer Butler followed suit in 2018.

All fine and good, but did they get their own *tram*? Well, Ozzy did.

In 2016, a Birmingham tram called the *Ozzy Osbourne* was christened, and none other than Ozzy Osbourne rode the *Ozzy Osbourne* on its maiden voyage from Corporation Square to New Street. According to the *New Music Express*, the crowd gathered for the festivities was chanting "Ozzy, Ozzy, Ozzy! Oi, oi, oi!" as the singer made an emotional speech.

"It's a great honor to have a tram named after me," he said. "I'm proud to be a Brummie and this means so much."

The tram line itself had been open since 1999 but still had yet to turn a profit. Initial estimates were that the tram would serve eight million people a year, but in reality, it was five million. While the tram was probably not named after the singer specifically to address the shortage of commuters, a document published by West Midlands Travel Trends in 2017 said that since the launch of the *Ozzy Osbourne*, ridership had reached the level required to meet initial projections.

"In a further boost to the Metro, patronage on the line between Birmingham and Wolverhampton city centers is at an all-time high—7.89 million passengers took the tram between June 2016 and May 2017."

Ozzy Osbourne returns to Birmingham in 2007 to receive his Walk of Stars award. The real winner is clearly the dude on the right who gets to wear that outfit.

68

OZZY & JACK'S WORLD DETOUR

THE OSBOURNES RETURN TO THE BOOB TUBE

JULY 24, 2016

The Osbourne family made its triumphant return to television in 2016 with *Ozzy & Jack's World Detour*. This reality show premiered on the History Channel for its first season, an appropriate choice considering that Ozzy spent much of his time on *The Osbournes* watching documentaries about Nazi Germany on that same network. The show moved to A&E for its second and third seasons.

In each episode, the singer and his son Jack would visit various sites of historical import. In the series premiere, the two visit Jamestown, where they're fitted for wigs. Then in the second episode, the pair visit the Alamo, the site of one of the Prince of Darkness's most legendary pee-pee adventures of the 1980s. During the rest of the season, they visit such sites as Mount Rushmore, Roswell, and Philadelphia's Mütter Museum of medical oddities, home of the world's largest human colon.

The Mütter Museum episode takes place on Ozzy's birthday, and there is a genuinely sweet moment in which he gets a video call from the un-Ozzy herself, Dolly Parton, whom he refers to as "my old friend." It would sure be interesting to see the origin story of that friendship. Anyway, she sings him "Happy Birthday" in her inimitable voice, then pulls Sharon into the frame for a hug. Ozzy declares it "the nicest part of the day," and it's clear that he's sincerely touched by the gesture.

The show lost some viewers when it moved to A&E for the next two seasons. At its peak in the first season, it pulled in 1.31 million viewers, according to *Showbuzz Daily*. It never reached those heights again, but it still did respectably enough, getting approximately three-quarters of a million viewers at its pinnacle.

The show's popularity was due to the fact that it was very entertaining. This is particularly true of season two when Ozzy meets Mac Sabbath, a Black Sabbath cover band who dress up as McDonaldland characters, such as Grimace, the Hamburglar, and Mayor

Jack does a presser for *World Detour*, 2016.

The mighty Mac Sabbath, who perform Black Sabbath classics while dressed as McDonaldland characters, performing in 2017. Whatever your belief system, you must agree that Mac Sabbath are doing the lord's work.

McCheese. Osbourne is clearly touched and entertained, and when he poses for a photo with the band, you can almost see the shit-eating grins on the faces of the band members, even those whose faces are obscured by a giant hamburger mask.

Daughter Kelly got involved in the show during season three, as Jack's time was frequently consumed with the birth of his daughter. The show wrapped up on August 8, 2018, and the final episode depicted Kelly getting a chocolate bust made of her famous father.

The show went off the air after season three, but in 2020, all three seasons were picked up by AXS TV, a network that shows all kinds of programming provided it's about rock music or wrestling. If you cannot get this channel through your local cable provider, you will be pleased to know that most of the craziest moments from the show are all over YouTube.

THIS IS
THE END

RIP BLACK SABBATH
(1968–2017)

MARCH 7, 2017

The Sabs employ a decorative curtain reminding their most stoned fans who they've shown up to see.

Few bands in history have had more breakups, reformations, regroupings, and other general instability than Black Sabbath. Despite having a steady lineup for its first decade, Ozzy's ouster in 1979 led to a decades-long period in which it was hard to say who was in the band, who wasn't, or if the band even still existed at all.

The 2011 reunion of the original lineup did a lot to make Black Sabbath seem like a real band again. While they had created a lot of great music in the band's many different configurations, the sense that the original, Ozzy-led lineup was the "real" one never went away. There was always a sense among fans that the original lineup needed to reunite, tour, and make a new album to end the Sabbath story properly.

While drummer Bill Ward didn't participate in the reunion, seeing Osbourne onstage, flanked by Iommi and Butler, was something a lot of fans believed would never happen again. Then it did, and after the well-received *13* album and the tour to support it, there began to be talk of the group maybe making another album, followed by one last tour.

Discussing a possible new album, Osbourne told *Metal Hammer* that the 2011 reunion had been an incredibly positive experience. They were all older and more mature, and they knew the window of opportunity was closing, so they got down to business.

"The whole Sabbath experience this time around was great," Ozzy said. "We all made friends, we didn't fuck around, we all knew

Black Sabbath at the end of *The End*, graciously telling the audience it's time to sod off.

that we had a job to do, and we did it. It was a lot of fun. So we're going to do one more album, and a final tour."

Although plans for a new album began to move forward, going as far as the enlistment of producer Rick Rubin to guide the sessions again, it didn't happen. Another world tour, however, did go forward. If anyone wondered if there would be another chance to see the band some other time in the future, Black Sabbath disabused such people of this notion by helpfully naming the tour *The End*.

If there was any complaint to be had with the tour, it was that the setlist remained pretty static, focusing almost entirely on the first four albums. Apparently, no one minded hearing "Iron Man" or "Paranoid"

for the billionth time, since *Blabbermouth* reported that "grosses from Black Sabbath's year-long farewell tour are estimated to be in the $100 million range, with more than a million tickets sold worldwide."

The tour ended fittingly in the band's hometown of Birmingham in February 2017. Osbourne admitted to the *BBC* that arriving at the venue for the last time was bittersweet.

"Since I've got to this building today, I've been happy, I've been tearful," he conceded. He also told *The Pulse of Radio* that the tour had gone a long way toward helping him put the past in the past for good.

"To come back and be friends with my buddies who I started off with all those

years ago, it's a closure for me, a chapter of my life which I can say, 'Well, we came, we saw, we had a good time and now it's over,'" he said. "I'm glad we ended up happy."

If anyone thought the end of the farewell tour would mean that the group would embark on a reunion tour the following year, the band permanently put the kibosh on such speculation on March 7, 2017, when they posted a very simple graphic to their official Facebook page. It featured the band's name as it was styled on the cover of their 1971 *Master of Reality* album, with "1968–2017" beneath it. It was captioned with the simple hashtag #TheEnd.

70

"NO MORE TOURS II"

THE MOST OFT-POSTPONED TOUR IN OZZYANITY

APRIL 27, 2018

Ozzy in Buenos Aires in 2018 on the frequently postponed "No More Tours II" tour. In fact, if you're reading this book in the year 3000, he may still have postponed dates to make up.

In May of 2017, Ozzy Osbourne announced that he would be embarking on a worldwide excursion known as the "No More Tours II" tour. He didn't rule out the possibility of one-off shows or some other low-commitment configuration of concerts at some point in the future, but when it came to dragging his nearly seventy-year-old self from one corner of the globe to another and back again for a year or more, he was done, and he meant it this time.

At the time of the announcement, the future showed no signs of anything that should stop him, for example, something like an injury or a global pandemic. But the Black Sabbath reunion and tour had come to an end, and now he intended to close the book on his solo career in a similarly triumphant fashion.

The tour started well enough, winding its way through North America, South America, Europe, and Israel. Even a staph infection didn't stop him, with *Rolling Stone* reporting that his return to the Ozzfest stage in Los Angeles on New Year's Eve of 2018 was "earlier than expected."

Despite the rosy prognosis, Ozzy soon entered a period in which he just couldn't catch a break. In April 2019, a statement on his official Instagram account said that he had fallen in his home, which

aggravated other, older injuries he had sustained in an ATV accident in 2003.

"Ozzy will postpone all his 2019 tour dates, inclusive of shows in North America and Europe, as he recovers from an injury sustained while dealing with his recent bout of pneumonia," the announcement said. However, he assured fans that he would be back, and we would see his triumphant return to the concert stage in 2020.

For reasons that everyone on Earth should be well acquainted with by now, he did not resume touring in 2020. The tour dates that were still outstanding got postponed more than once as he dealt with his own recovery and as it became clear that the COVID-19 pandemic was not going to go away any time soon. Then, in November 2021, it was announced that the remaining tour dates had been postponed yet again, this time getting pushed back to 2023.

It was a tough blow for fans and singer alike, but thanks to the sleuthing of the

good people at *NME*, a nugget of good news was unearthed. According to a document from Osbourne's label Sony with the mellifluous and easy-to-remember name "Supplemental Information for the Consolidated Financial Results for the Second Quarter Ended September 30, 2021," Ozzy would take these dire circumstances and use them to his advantage by recording a new album.

The then-unfinished and untitled album would be bittersweet to hear. It features drumming contributions from the late Taylor Hawkins of Foo Fighters, who died in 2022 from a drug overdose.

"TAKE WHAT YOU WANT"

OZZY TEAMS WITH POST MALONE TO THE CHAGRIN OF SOME

OCTOBER 15, 2019

In 1988, Ozzy Osbourne engaged in an act that many diehard fans considered nothing less than blasphemy. He performed a duet with Lita Ford on a song called "Close My Eyes Forever," and it was a *power ballad*, the lowest form of musical entertainment in all of recorded history. It was considered an act of selling out that was so unforgivable that it should have caused whatever deity in charge to smite the entire human race with an asteroid twice the size of the one that killed the dinosaurs.

Despite the wailing and lamentations of Ozzy's fans, he was eventually forgiven for this terrible transgression and continued his solo career unimpeded. But while he had been forgiven, this unfortunate indiscretion could never be forgotten. If at any time in the future Osbourne were to try to get on the charts yet again by teaming up with some artist whose music was insufficiently grim and dark and forbidding, he would pay the ultimate price.

Apparently, the "ultimate price" was just more bitching. In 2019, he provided guest vocals on the song "Take What You Want" by rapper Post Malone, which featured contributions by rapper Travis Scott. The song featured writing contributions from all three of them, so you couldn't really argue that Osbourne wasn't fully invested in it or was just cashing in on some trend.

Many people tried to, but the argument didn't hold up to close scrutiny. First and foremost, the song is really not bad. If you removed the rapping and drum machines and let a live band perform it behind him instead, it's very easy to picture the song passing muster with any Ozzy fan. If there's any reason to be upset about it, it's more that Osbourne doesn't have a whole lot to do on the song after the first verse, in which he sings lead.

Malone told New Zealand DJ Zane Lowe that he was not in the studio when Ozzy recorded his parts with producer Andrew Watt. However, he said the producer had said to him that the project was gratifying to the singer.

"I mean, he was talking to Watt and Watt was telling me he was like this, 'Yo, this is my favorite that I've done since, you know, Sabbath, and since I started my own, own way,'" Malone said. "I was like, 'That's huge. I'm like honored. Thank you very much.'"

Not everyone was entirely on board with Osbourne's rosy assessment of the song. Henry Yates wrote in *Classic Rock* that it had been hopelessly embellished with "icy electronic beats jarring horribly," and some of the more purist members of the hard rock and heavy metal community would have likely preferred to pretend the whole thing had never happened.

Despite the haters, the song provided a small moment of career déjà vu for Osbourne. "Take What You Want" debuted at #8 on the *Billboard* Hot 100, and the singer had not appeared on a Top 10 single in decades. Three decades, to be precise. The last time he had was in 1989 when "Close My Eyes Forever" with Lita Ford charted at #8.

Ozzy at the 2019 American Music Awards with Post Malone, with whom he committed the unpardonable sin of getting a song on the radio.

PART 7

LIVIN' LA VIDA LOCKDOWN, 2020–2022

Ozzy performs at the 2022 Commonwealth Games in Birmingham, his first show after major surgery had been performed on his neck. And Tony Iommi was there!

72

PARDON MY PARKINSON'S

OZZY GETS A CENTRAL NERVOUS SYSTEM DISORDER

JANUARY 21, 2020

It was 2020. It was a new year, a new decade, and as far as anyone knew, there would be nothing remarkable that would happen in, say, mid-March. Perhaps confident that no one would swoop in and take up valuable airtime by discussing airborne pathogens, Ozzy went on *Good Morning America* with Sharon at his side to reveal that he had been diagnosed with Parkinson's disease in February 2019.

"It's PRKN 2," Sharon explained to journalist Robin Roberts. "There's so many different types of Parkinson's; it's not a death sentence by any stretch of the imagination, but it does affect certain nerves in your body.... It's like you have a good day, a good day, and then a really bad day."

Ozzy had been through Parkinson's scares before, such as when he was screened for it in 1992, but he had never received the actual diagnosis. This time, he not only got the diagnosis, but he got it while dealing with the after-effects of a surgical procedure. It was not a good time to be diagnosed with a progressive disorder with no cure, to put it mildly.

"I had a bad fall," he said. "I had to have surgery on my neck, which screwed all my nerves."

He explained that he began to have alarming physical sensations after his surgery. The most disturbing part was that he couldn't tell if the sensations were after-effects of the surgery or side effects of Parkinson's disease.

"I got a numbness down this arm for the surgery, my legs keep going cold," the singer said. "I don't know if that's the Parkinson's or what.... Because they cut nerves when they did the surgery. I'd never heard of nerve pain, and it's a weird feeling."

Osbourne said that his children had realized something was wrong and sounded the alarm. Daughter Kelly described the situation as "a role reversal" and conceded that it had taken some time for everyone in the family to view the situation in the same way. His son Jack, who had been diagnosed with multiple sclerosis in 2012, said that he felt his situation was similar to his father's, and he could relate.

As for the man himself, he said that it was an "adjustment" to find himself in the role of needing to lean on his family. He said he had been brought up in an environment where dads didn't do that because their fundamental purpose was to be the primary breadwinner. Watching his wife and adult children go out and be productive members of society while he convalesced at home starkly contrasted with how he was brought up.

"Coming from a working-class background, I hate to let people down. I hate to not do my job," he said. "And so when I see my wife goin' to work, my kids goin' to work, everybody's doing—tryin' to be helpful to me, that gets me down because I can't contribute to my family, you know."

The famous celebrity duo who performed the smash 2003 cover of Black Sabbath's "Changes" appear at the Grammy Awards. Those two are going places.

73

ORDINARY MAN

OZZY'S FIRST NEW ALBUM IN TEN YEARS GETS DOWN TO BUSINESS

FEBRUARY 21, 2020

It would be grotesque and unseemly to suggest that Ozzy Osbourne's revelation of his Parkinson's diagnosis was just a publicity stunt meant to bring attention to *Ordinary Man*, his first solo album in ten years. Perish the thought. Having said that, the timing didn't suck, and having a full-court press at the time of the album's release meant it would definitely get some newspaper ink.

The album was produced by Andrew Watt and Louis Bell and features Duff McKagan of Guns N' Roses on bass and Chad Smith of the Red Hot Chili Peppers on drums. The guitars were played mainly by Watt, although Tom Morello of Rage Against the Machine and Slash make their own contributions. It was released in early 2020, just a few months after Osbourne's collaboration with Post Malone, "Take What You Want," had returned him to the charts.

That song appears as a bonus track on some configurations of this album, as well as a second collaboration between the two, "It's a Raid." Purist fans who groused at "Take What You Want" were likely none too pleased to find a second collaboration with Post Malone on the album, but what really must have rankled them was the title track, which features guest vocals and piano by Elton John.

It was a more fitting pairing than fans might have realized. The lyrics openly state that both men have cheated death on numerous occasions, with Elton John famously having a roaring appetite for cocaine back in the day. The pairing may have been unexpected, but it was justified.

As for the rest of the album, it's the best thing to carry Osbourne's name as a solo

On the Sirius XM show *Ozzy's Boneyard*, Birmingham's favorite son sits between producer Andrew Watt and guitarist Billy Morrison in 2020. Would it kill them to use drink coasters?

artist in a long time. While some of the production choices are a little too slick, it works well overall, and a few of the songs, such as "Straight to Hell" and "Under the Graveyard," actually rock pretty damn hard. While Morello and Slash contribute some excellent guitar playing to the album, Andrew Watt's riffs and rhythms give it its muscle, and they don't let up.

Osbourne has never been a critic's darling, but journalists gave *Ordinary Man* high marks this time. Fred Thomas of *AllMusic* hit the nail on the head when he said, "The production is huge, but the energy is spontaneous . . . the better songs here rank among his best."

If the reviews are a bummer in any respect, it's that a lot of them seem less like album reviews and more like obituaries. Josh Gray's review in *Clash* wrapped up with a compliment that reads more like a eulogy.

"*Ordinary Man* is far from perfect," he wrote. "It does, however, absolutely succeed on its own terms, serving its purpose by reminding the world just what we'll miss when this titan among titans finally departs us for good."

Ozzy must have been aware that the critics were measuring him for a coffin. Rather than let *Ordinary Man* be his swan song and a prelude to him shuffling off this mortal coil, *Rolling Stone* reported

on February 25, 2020—four days after *Ordinary Man*'s release date—that the singer was already recording his next album. Sadly, *Urinating on the Graves of My Detractors* was not the title he would ultimately choose for it.

74

OZZY AND JACK'S ADVENTURES WITH SOBRIETY

THE OSBOURNE DUDES REMAIN LUCID

FEBRUARY 5, 2021

During the social-distancing era of the COVID-19 pandemic, when there was no vaccine and things were dire, many people dealt with the stress and anxiety the same way they tolerate relatives at Thanksgiving, with heavy drinking. The blog of Cedars-Sinai Medical Center in Los Angeles published the findings of a September 2020 RAND Corporation study, and they were grim.

"Alcohol consumption rose among adults over age 30 by 14% during the pandemic," the blog said. So it is perhaps wryly amusing to note that while many people were facing down the apocalypse by getting shitfaced, two people who weren't were Ozzy Osbourne and his son Jack. The two men were joined by Sharon for an interview with Marc Malkin of *Variety*, in which they revealed that the singer had been sober for seven years, while Jack had been sober for seventeen.

Sharon revealed that far from fearing that Ozzy was modeling behavior their children would emulate later in life, she thought it would have the opposite effect. She believed, understandably, that seeing their father blackout drunk in a puddle of his own bodily fluids would deter them from ever picking up a bottle. She conceded that she had gotten that one wrong.

"I was like, 'This is really like a huge, huge life lesson for them,'" she recalled. "'They'll never be like this because look, this guy's pissing himself on the floor. This one's throwing up. This one's just got a divorce. And their behavior's outrageous. There's no way they will follow this.' And they kept seeing their dad go back into rehab, and back, and back. And so I just thought, 'They won't want this in their life.'"

She also revealed that worrying about her husband's well-being had been an all-day, every-day, full-time job for her. Malkin asked how many times she thought her husband might die, and she said

that it was less a specific number of times and more of a constant state that she was in at all times.

"I was terrified that he was going to get sick in the night, or fall over, hit his head," she said. "I would always make sure that there was somebody there, checking on him through the night when he was on the road without me. But it was always in the front of my mind."

Ozzy said that when he was drinking, he wasn't concerned about what kind of an example he was setting for his family or what he was putting them through. He said that's just the nature of being an addict—everyone has to care except for the addict.

"I didn't give a shit, because I was loaded," he said. "It's a very selfish disease. You don't think about it because you're loaded, in an altered state."

Jack went into treatment while *The Osbournes* was being filmed. Despite being only seventeen years old when he made the decision, he was able to tell that the way his treatment was playing out in public was "incredibly invasive and, morally, really inappropriate." At the time of the *Variety* interview, Malkin reminded the younger Osbourne that with seventeen years of sobriety behind him, he could now say he had been continuously sober for half of his life.

"That's just great, Jack," Ozzy said. "I'm really proud of you for that."

They're tanned, rested, and ready. Ozzy and Jack Osbourne at the premiere of *God Bless Ozzy Osbourne* at the 2011 Tribeca Film Festival.

75

OZZY AND SHARON GET COVID

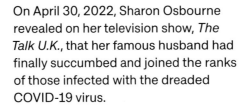

MAYBE THEY SHOULD HAVE TRIED IVERMECTIN

MAY 5, 2022

On April 30, 2022, Sharon Osbourne revealed on her television show, *The Talk U.K.*, that her famous husband had finally succumbed and joined the ranks of those infected with the dreaded COVID-19 virus.

"I am very worried about Ozzy right now," she revealed. "We've gone two years without him catching COVID and it's just Ozzy's luck he would get it now."

Ever the supportive spouse, Sharon said that she would take some time from the television show to go home and be with her ailing husband. Saying that she would "hold him and kiss him with about three masks on," she didn't anticipate being gone for very long.

"It will take me a week to get my old man back on his feet again and I will be back in a week," she said resolutely.

Unfortunately, germs did what germs do, and the novel SARS-CoV-2 virus particles that had taken up residence in Ozzy's airways infected his wife. She shared her disease status via her Instagram account, and rather than spin a long yarn about it, the entire caption consisted of one word— "Covid"—which was flanked by two frowny face emojis. She later revealed that it wasn't just her that had it, either.

"My daughter Kelly now has it, and I have it," she said in a video posted to her Instagram account. "And the entire household has it now."

The video's comments section was flooded with good tidings from well-wishers, one of whom remarked that she was "much stronger than COVID." Surprising absolutely no one, she reported that her husband, whom she had gone home to tend to, was coming along perfectly fine.

"He's doing much better," she said. "His temperature's now back to normal."

Jack was unaffected by the virus and took it upon himself to keep fans updated on how everyone was doing.

"Dad is on the mend and still FaceTiming the dogs," Jack said. "Thank you for all the love & support!"

According to *Rolling Stone*, it was not Sharon or Kelly's first time with the illness. Sharon first tested positive for the virus in December 2020. While the publication said it was "not exactly clear" when Kelly had first succumbed, writer Jon Blistein noted that in March 2021, she had begun using the hashtag #StayHomeforOzzy to encourage people to keep those at high risk safe from the virus.

Tragically, the fact that Ozzy Osbourne got COVID-19 means that his theory for why he never got it before has now been disproven. In October 2021, Dr. Osbourne gave his hypothesis as to why he was as yet uninfected while those around him succumbed to the illness.

"My wife had the virus; my daughter had the virus and I never got it," he told *Metal Hammer*. "Being a devil worshipper does have its good points!"

Ozzy and Sharon attend a pre-Grammy
event in The Before Times, January 25, 2020.

75.666

PATIENT NUMBER 9

OZZY MAKES ANOTHER ALBUM, AND THE HATERS CAN SUCK IT

SEPTEMBER 9, 2022

For decades, every Ozzy Osbourne album that was released was believed by many to be his last. He had tempted fate too many times, snorted too many live ants, and urinated on too many cenotaphs to remain forever in the lord's good favor. It was just a matter of time before it caught up with him, and there was little doubt that his final album would be posthumous.

Well, on September 9, 2022, he released his thirteenth studio album, *Patient Number 9*, and when it was released, he was still alive. It comes hot on the heels of 2020's *Ordinary Man*, which is quick by 2022 standards. Even Ozzy himself had not released anything as a solo artist in the decade following 2010's *Scream*. However, he said at the time of *Ordinary Man*'s release that the sessions had gone so well and been so productive that he immediately started work on his next album, and *Patient Number 9* is the final product. The album is a star-studded affair featuring turns by Tony Iommi and Zakk Wylde, as well as such less likely collaborators as Jeff Beck and former Enoch Powell supporter Eric Clapton.

Stylistically, it picks up where *Ordinary Man* left off, even using producer Andrew Watt again. Clearly, Watt is an excellent foil for Osbourne, who has a sense of purpose on this album that many people may have believed he just didn't have in him anymore.

The production still shimmers like its predecessor, but *Patient Number 9* is heavier while still being accessible. "Mr. Darkness" has plenty of Sabbath-inspired riffing, and Wylde unleashes his usual mayhem on the guitar solo. The following track, "Nothing Feels Right," is the greatest song Type O Negative never recorded, and "Degradation Rules" marks the triumphant return of the harmonica to an Ozzy recording, the first since "The Wizard" on Black Sabbath's debut.

The album isn't a full-fledged return to the crushing heaviness of Black Sabbath. Still, in fairness, no Ozzy solo album ever was. But it's engaging, engrossing, and never boring. It's clear when you listen to it that Osbourne enjoyed working with Watt a great deal, and even all the studio trickery that was undoubtedly involved in making this album doesn't obscure that. His enjoyment is palpable, and it's the biggest reason why this album works as well as it does.

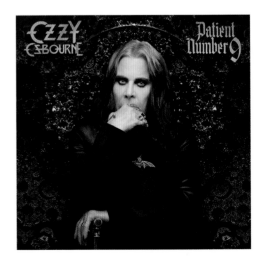

The album received good reviews upon its release. Dom Lawson of *Louder Sound* wrote that the album was "really, really good" and awarded it four stars out of five.

"Ozzy has conjured some of his strongest material in decades," he wrote. "Despite everything you may have heard about Ozzy being on his last legs, *Patient Number 9* unequivocally does not sound like the work of a man living on borrowed time. Instead, it sounds like the Prince of fucking Darkness having an absolutely smashing time, with a bunch of his mates and, weirdly, a newfound sense of artistic ambition."

He ain't wrong. *Patient Number 9* is a surprisingly strong album that proves yet again that anyone betting against Ozzy Osbourne will lose, and lose badly.

Ozzy performs at the halftime show at the NFL Kickoff Game in 2022. For reasons best known to them, the NBC network cut away from his performance after less than ten seconds.

INDEX

BIBLIOGRAPHY

BOOKS

Iommi, Tony. *Iron Man: My Journey through Heaven and Hell with Black Sabbath*. Boston: Da Capo Press, 2011.

Lee, Tommy, Mick Mars, Vince Neil, and Nikki Sixx. *The Dirt: Confessions of the World's Most Notorious Rock Band*. New York: HarperCollins, 2001.

Osbourne, Ozzy. *I Am Ozzy*. New York: Grand Central Publishing, 2010.

Rosen, Steven. *The Story of Black Sabbath: Wheels of Confusion*. Chessington: Castle Communications, 1996.

Sarzo, Rudy. *Off the Rails: Aboard the Crazy Train in the Blizzard of Ozz*. New York: TooSmart! Publishing, 2008.

Wall, Mick. *Black Sabbath: Symptom of the Universe*. New York: St. Martin's Press, 2013.

ARTICLES

Adalian, Josef. "The Osbournes: Over and Out at Fox," thewrap.com, August 6, 2009.

Barton, Geoff. "Ozzy Osbourne: My Life Story," loudersound.com, October 4, 2016.

Begrand, Adrien. "Ozzy Osbourne: Blizzard of Ozz / Diary of a Madman," popmatters.com, June 24, 2002.

Blistein, Jon. "Thank the Dark Lord: Ozzy Osbourne Credits Devil Worship for Warding Off Covid-19," *Rolling Stone*, October 11, 2021.

Brannigan, Paul. "World Exclusive: Black Sabbath to Record New Album," loudersound.com, September 29, 2014.

Cartwright, Garth. "Don Arden," *Guardian*, July 25, 2007.

Catlin, Roger. "'Osbournes Reloaded': Worst Variety Show Ever?", *Hartford Courant*, March 31, 2009.

De Leaumont, Don. "Blast from the Past: Ozzy Osbourne/Type O Negative/Sepultura—May 18, 1996—Atlanta, GA," southeastofheaven.com, September 26, 2012.

Desta, Yohana. "The Dirt: Did Ozzy Osbourne Really Snort Ants and Drink His Own Urine?", *Vanity Fair*, March 22, 2019.

Earls, John. "Ozzy Osbourne Has a Tram Named After Him in Birmingham," *NME*, May 27, 2016.

Eddy, Chuck. "Ozzmosis," *Entertainment Weekly*, November 24, 1995.

Elliott, Paul. "At War, Unravelling and Flying High: How Black Sabbath Made Sabotage," loudersound.com, April 14, 2021.

Emeritus, Mikesn. "Ozzy Osbourne: Black Rain," sputnikmusic.com, May 22, 2007.

Fischer, Michael. "On Yer Bike with Studio Wizard Max Norman," knac.com, June 19, 2007.

France, Lisa Respers. "Ozzy Osbourne Is Postponing All His 2019 Concert Dates After an Illness and an Injury," cnn.com, April 5, 2019.

Fulton, Rick. "'I Was Stoned Every Day While Filming *The Osbournes*, Admits Ozzy Osbourne," *Daily Record*, May 4, 2009.

Genet, Danielle, and Angeline Jane Bernabe. "Ozzy Osbourne Breaks His Silence on His Battle with Parkinson's Disease," goodmorningamerica.com, January 21, 2020.

Gittins, Ian. "'Eminem Sings About Killing His Wife. My Husband Actually Tried to Do It,'" *Guardian*, May 25, 2001.

Graham, Jane. "Ozzy Osbourne: A Letter to My Younger Self," streetroots.org, January 4, 2015.

Graham, Jane. "Ozzy Osbourne Interview: 'I Tried a Bit of Burglary But I Was Useless,'" bigissue.com, November 3, 2014.

Gray, Josh. "Ozzy Osbourne—Ordinary Man," clashmusic.com, February 24, 2020.

Greene, Andy. "Ozzy Osbourne: Black Rain," *Rolling Stone*, May 15, 2007.

Grow, Kory, "Black Sabbath on the Making of 'Vol. 4': 'It Was Absolute Pandemonium,'" *Rolling Stone*, February 12, 2021.

Grow, Kory. "Fetus Jars and Werewolves: Ozzy Osbourne Looks Back Ahead of Box Set Release," *Rolling Stone*, August 23, 2019.

Grow, Kory. "Ozzy Osbourne Already Working on 'Ordinary Man' Follow-Up," *Rolling Stone*, February 25, 2020.

Grow, Kory. "Ozzy Osbourne Pays Tribute to Randy Rhoads: 'I Owe My Career to Him,'" *Rolling Stone*, May 18, 2021.

Grow, Kory. "Ozzy Osbourne, Recovering from Surgery, to Headline New Year's Eve Ozzfest," *Rolling Stone*, October 22, 2018.

Guest, Katy. "The Unusual Osbourne: Aimee Forsakes the Family Business to Find Her Own Way," *Independent*, February 24, 2008.

Hextall, Adrian. "Interview with FM Vocalist, Steve Overland," myglobalmind.com, March 14, 2015.

Hill, Karen. "Ozzy Osbourne, Kiss Tours Among Top 10 of 1996," *Billboard*, July 5, 2017.

Hutchison, Courtney. "Ozzy Osbourne Is a Genetic Mutant," abcnews.go.com, November 2, 2010.

Johnson, Kevin. "Black Sabbath's Reunion Tour Is Coming," notreble.com, November 20, 2011.

Johnson, Ross. "What I've Learned: Ozzy Osbourne," *Esquire*, January 1, 2005.

Johnston, Maura. "The 50 Worst Songs of the '00s," *Village Voice*, December 3, 2009.

Jonze, Tim. "Ozzy Osbourne: 'If I'd Have Gone to Church I'd Still Be There Now, Confessing All My Sins!,'" *GQ*, November 26, 2020.

Kaufman, Gil. "Black Sabbath Finally Make Rock Hall of Fame—Whether Ozzy Likes It or Not," mtv.com, November 28, 2005.

Kennedy, Helen, and Timothy J. Burger. "W Rocked by Ozzy at Dinner," *Daily News*, May 5, 2002.

Kilkelly, Daniel. "Osbourne Reflects on Childhood Trauma," digitalspy.com, March 7, 2007.

Kreps, Daniel. "New Ozzy Tracks Premiere In 'Rock Band,'" *Rolling Stone*, June 7, 2010.

Kreps, Daniel. "Ozzy Osbourne Tests Positive for Covid-19, But 'He's OK,' Sharon Says," *Rolling Stone*, April 28, 2022.

Kreps, Daniel. "Scientists Probe Ozzy's Body for Medical Miracles," *Rolling Stone*, June 15, 2010.

Lawson, Don. "Ozzy Osbourne's *Patient Number 9*: Metal's Greatest Icon Continues His Late-Career Hot Streak," loudersound.com, August 31, 2022.

Lester, Paul. "Black Sabbath: 'We Used to Have Cocaine Flown In by Private Plane,'" *Guardian*, June 6, 2013.

Malkin, Marc. "The Osbournes Open Up about Addiction and How the Family Finally Found Recovery," *Variety*, February 5, 2021.

Moore, Sam. "Ozzy Osbourne Was 'Blown Away' by His Invitation to the White House in 2002," *NME*, September 8, 2020.

Munson, Kyle. "Ozzy Left His Mark," *Des Moines Register*, December 19, 2007.

Oliver, Mark. "Rock'n'roll Ozzy Hurt in Quad-Bike Accident," *Guardian*, December 9, 2003.

Parker, Lyndsey. "Bassist Rudy Sarzo Remembers Ozzy Osbourne's Bat-Biting, 40 Years Later: 'Sharon Knew Immediately That She Had an Opportunity Here,'" yahoo.com, January 20, 2022.

Patterson, Charmaine. "Sharon Osbourne Says She Has COVID-19 as She Shares Photo of Her in Bed with an IV," *People*, May 4, 2022.

Philips, Chuck. "Harsh Reality of 'Osbournes' No Laughing Matter," *Los Angeles Times*, December 7, 2003.

Reesman, Bryan. "Digital Playlist: Rob Halford," bryanreesman.com, November 16, 2011.

Reiher, Andrea. "Ozzy Osbourne on 1st Wife Thelma: 'I Treated Her Really Badly,'" heavy.com, September 7, 2020.

Roberts, Randall. "When Jimmy Carter's White House Was a Tour Stop for Long-Haired, 'Torpedo'-Smoking Rock Outlaws," *Los Angeles Times*, September 9, 2020.

Runtagh, Jordan. "The Eagles' 'Hotel California': 10 Things You Didn't Know," *Rolling Stone*, December 8, 2016.

Ruskell, Nick. "Album Review: Black Sabbath—Sabotage Super Deluxe," *Kerrang*, June 11, 2021.

Scapelliti, Christopher. "Geezer Butler: Black Sabbath's 'Paranoid' Sounded Like a Led Zeppelin Rip-Off," *Guitar World*, September 27, 2016.

Schleinkofer, Gabriella. "Ozzy Osbourne: The Godfather of Metal," deathmetal.org, June 2002.

Schruers, Fred. "Sharon and Ozzy Osbourne's House in Los Angeles," *Architectural Digest*, June 2011.

Sprague, David. "Rock and Roll Hall of Fame 2006: Black Sabbath," *Rolling Stone*, March 6, 2006.

Susman, Gary. "Ozzy Osbourne Reveals Childhood Sexual Abuse," *Entertainment Weekly*, December 1, 2003.

Susman, Gary. "Sharon Osbourne Says Her Cancer Has Spread," *Entertainment Weekly*, July 19, 2002.

Tan, Emily. "Ozzy Osbourne and Post Malone Join Forces On 'It's a Raid,'" *Spin*, February 20, 2020.

Tolinski, Brad, and Alan Paul. "Tony Iommi and James Hetfield Discuss Their Guitar Journeys with Black Sabbath and Metallica in This Classic 1992 Guitar World Interview," *Guitar World*, August 1992.

Trueheart, Charles. "Elvis' Secret Offer to Nixon," *Washington Post*, September 20, 1988.

Turman, Katherine. "Tony Iommi Looks Back at Black Sabbath, Meeting Dio and His Friendship with Eddie Van Halen," *Spin*, March 11, 2021.

Vineyard, Jennifer. "Ozzy Osbourne Opens Up About the Bad Old Days in New Film," *Rolling Stone*, April 27, 2011.

Wells, Troy. "Don Airey: The Ballbuster Interview," ballbustermusic.com, March 2004.

Wiederhorn, Jon. "40 Years Ago: Ozzy Osbourne Arrested for Urinating on Alamo Cenotaph," loudwire.com, February 19, 2022.

Wiederhorn, Jon. "Ozzy Osbourne Fans Scream Into the Guinness Book of World Records," noisecreep.com, June 17, 2010.

Wilkening, Matthew. "Revisiting Ozzy Osbourne's 'Suicide Solution' Lawsuit," ultimateclassicrock.com, October 26, 2015.

Witter, Brad. "The 10 Most Outrageous Moments from 'The Osbournes,'" biography.com, June 29, 2018.

Yates, Henry. "Ozzy Osbourne's Ordinary Man: Anything but Ordinary," loudersound.com, February 21, 2020.

WEBSITES

allmusic.com

billboard.com

billward.com

birminghammail.co.uk

blabbermouth.net

bobdaisley.com

cheatsheet.com

corporate.tfwm.org.uk

jamanetwork.com

loudersound.com

ozzy.com

pagesix.com

showbuzzdaily.com

sony.com

thetimes.co.uk

IMAGE CREDITS

A = all, B = bottom, L = left, R = right, T = top

Alamy Stock Photos: 10, Richard Franklin; 11, Dave Bagnall Collection; 12, Stoxo; 13, Mirrorpix; 14, FLPA; 15, Mirrorpix; 19TR, Smith Archive; 31, Mirrorpix; 34, Mirrorpix; 46, marka/press holland; 47, marka/press holland; 51T, Mirrorpix; 54–55A, Bill Waterson; 62, Mirrorpix; 68–69, Media Punch; 77, Media Punch; 79, ZUMA Press; 80, John Atashian; 84–85, Mirrorpix; 86, Media Punch; 91T, Media Punch; 96, Media Punch; 106, Mirrorpix; 113, Media Punch; 120T, Media Punch; 122, Media Punch; 129, AJ Pics; 130, Media Punch; 141, Featureflash Archive; 145, Mirrorpix; 148, Newscast Online; 155, Jarle H. Moe; 157, Andrew Winning; 158, ZUMA; 161, dpa; 162, GTCRFOTO; 163, Tim Ockenden; 164, David McNew; 167, Terje Dokken; 168, PA; 169, Edward Moss; 171, Ken Howard; 174, Nestor J. Beremblum; 175T, Nestor J. Beremblum; 179, David Davies; 181, ZUMA; 185, WENN; 187, Media Punch; 200, Media Punch; back endpapers, Terje Dokken.

Robert Alford: 52, 56, 88, 89, 92–93A, 98, 99.

AP Newsroom: 95, Lacy Atkins; 107, AP Photo; 151, Jeff Christensen.

Creative Commons: 24, Pixabay (CC0); 150T, Christina Spicuzza (CCA-SA 2.0 Generic); 172, Steve Knight (CC by 2.0); 173, Steve Knight (CC by 2.0).

Getty Images: Front endpapers, 4, Fin Costello/Redferns; 4, Fin Costello/Redferns; 7, Fin Costello/Redferns; 9, Ellen Poppinga – K&K/Redferns; 17, Ellen Poppinga – K&K/Redferns; 21, Chris Walter/WireImage; 23, Chris Walter/WireImage; 25, Michael Ochs Archives; 26, Michael Putland/Hulton Archive; 28–29, Chris Walter/WireImage; 33, Chris Walter/WireImage; 37, Chris Walter/WireImage; 38, Michael Putland/Hulton Archive; 43, Michael Putland/Hulton Archive; 44–45, Chris Walter/WireImage; 59, Gus Stewart/Redferns; 63, Dave Hogan/Hulton Archive; 64–65, Fin Costello/Redferns; 71, Fin Costello/Redferns; 73, Watal Asanuma/Shinko Music/Hulton Archive; 101, Paul Natkin; 109, Koh Hesebe/Shinko Music/Hulton Archive; 115, Mick Hutson/Redferns; 116, Mick Hutson/Redferns; 119T, Martyn Goodacre/Hulton Archive; 127L, Simon Ritter/Redferns; 133, Mick Hutson/Redferns; 134, Getty Images Entertainment; 138, Paul J. Richards/AFP; 139, Theo Wargo/WireImage; 142, Jonathan Daniel; 147, MJ Kim; 149, Getty Images Entertainment; 165, Lester Cohen/WireImage; 170, Monica Schipper/WireImage; 177, Emma McIntyre/AMA 2019; 183, Kevin Winter; 189, Icon Sportswire.

Dean Messina/Frank White Photo Agency: 61.

Stephen Rossini/Frank White Photo Agency: 2.

Shutterstock: 16, Bohbeh; 36, Roman Peleshko; 40, Walter Cicchetti; 50, Malshak; 51B, Sirocco; 58, monticello; 70, photomaster; 90, asharkyu; 143, karamysh; 160, LoopAll.

Laurens Van Houten/Frank White Photo Agency: 41, 49.

Frank White: 66, 67L, 74, 83, 103, 104, 110, 124, 137, 152.

ACKNOWLEDGMENTS

My name may be on the spine of this book, but I couldn't have done this by myself. I'm very grateful to Constance Brinkley-Badgett and Amy Vernon, both of whom were employing me, and John Kane, my co-host on the *Two Guys Talking Rush* podcast. Your support and encouragement when I got this offer meant a lot to me.

I'm grateful to my parents, Albert and Joanna Bukszpan, and my sister Claudia Rutherford, who have been in my corner every step of the way as I've been a writer. Thanks to my mother-in-law Valborg Linn for covering my parental duties while I worked on this and for being an ongoing source of encouragement.

Huge thanks are due to Dennis Pernu of Motorbooks, who gave me this project. This was hands down the most enjoyable experience I've ever had writing anything. Yes, meeting deadlines and turning in good writing required seriousness, organization, and discipline on my part, but at no time did it ever feel like work. I loved every second of it.

Thanks to my son, Roman, for being the reason I pick projects that I like. When you get to be an old fart like me, I want you to find work that means something to you and makes you happy. I hope that while I've been working on this book, I was able to model that for you in some way.

Finally, thank you to my wife, Asia, the love of my life. You have always supported me, you have always stopped me from doing things that make me miserable, and you have always defined success as "doing something for a living that makes you happy." I would never have had a career as a writer without you. I owe you everything, and I love you more than anything.

ABOUT THE AUTHOR

Daniel Bukszpan has been a freelance writer for over 25 years. He has written for such publications as Fortune, CNBC, Condé Nast Traveler, and many more. He is the author of The Encyclopedia of Heavy Metal, The Encyclopedia of New Wave, The Art of Brutal Legend, and Woodstock: 50 Years of Peace and Music. He also contributed to AC/DC: High-Voltage Rock 'N' Roll, Iron Maiden: The Ultimate Unauthorized History of the Beast, Metallica: The Complete Illustrated History, and Rush: The Illustrated History. He lives in Brooklyn, New York, with his wife, Asia, and his son, Roman.

Quarto.com

© 2023 Quarto Publishing Group USA Inc.
Text © 2023 Daniel Bukszpan

First Published in 2023 by Motorbooks, an imprint of The Quarto Group,
100 Cummings Center, Suite 265-D, Beverly, MA 01915, USA.
T (978) 282-9590 F (978) 283-2742

Motorbooks titles are also available at discount for retail, wholesale, promotional, and bulk purchase. For details, contact the Special Sales Manager by email at specialsales@quarto.com or by mail at The Quarto Group, Attn: Special Sales Manager, 100 Cummings Center, Suite 265-D, Beverly, MA 01915, USA.

26 25 24 23   1 2 3 4 5

ISBN: 978-0-7603-7743-7

Digital edition published in 2023
eISBN: 978-0-7603-7744-4

Library of Congress Cataloging-in-Publication Data

Names: Bukszpan, Daniel, author.
Title: Ozzy at 75 / Daniel Bukszpan.
Description: Beverly, MA : Motorbooks, 2023. | Includes bibliographical references and index. |
Summary: "Ozzy at 75 celebrates the anniversary of the gonzo rock icon's birth with a beautifully produced retrospective of 75 key achievements and life events"-- Provided by publisher.
Identifiers: LCCN 2022061767 | ISBN 9780760377437 | ISBN 9780760377444 (ebook)
Subjects: LCSH: Osbourne, Ozzy, 1948- | Rock musicians--England--Biography. | Black Sabbath (Musical group)
Classification: LCC ML420.O825 B85 2023 | DDC 782.42166092 [B]--dc23/eng/20221223
LC record available at https://lccn.loc.gov/2022061767
Classification: LCC ML420.O825 B85 2023 | DDC 782.42166092 [B]--dc23/eng/20221223
LC record available at https://lccn.loc.gov/2022061767

Design: www.traffic-design.co.uk
Slipcase Image: Robert Alford
Book Cover Image: Martyn Goodacre/Getty Images
Page Layout: www.traffic-design.co.uk

Printed in China